What Is a Teacher?

What is a Teacher?

ORIGINAL TITLE: *Preface to Teaching*

HENRY W. SIMON

Revised and expanded with an introduction for this edition by John H. Fischer, President, Teachers College, Columbia University

COLLIER BOOKS *New York*

COLLIER-MACMILLAN LTD *London*

Introduction

Henry Adams' observation that a teacher can never tell where his influence stops is the truth, but only part of it. Aside from the duration of his influence it is almost as difficult for him to know even what kind of effect he has had. This is hard enough to judge after a single lesson. To guess what it might be after a semester—or ten years later—is well nigh impossible. The residue might be so slight it disappears at once. It may add a tiny increment to the student's slow accumulation of knowledge and assurance. But sometimes, in ways no one quite understands, a lecture, a sentence, or a single unplanned word may be the spark that lights a life-long flame.

Yet, for all the uncertainty, the echoes that return to one who has taught long enough to hear them can be impressively consistent. Almost invariably, if the teacher's influence has been good, what the student remembers is the attention that was paid to *him,* the respect his teacher accorded him. People can be taught—and can learn—without being respected, but the result is not education. It is more likely to be a kind of training, quite possibly effective and perhaps lasting, but hardly of the quality to give the student a heightened sense of his own capacities, or a desire to go, on his own, beyond the point at which his teacher leaves him. The difference between training and education is not uniformly recognized, even in schools where it should be. But a good teacher always knows the difference and much of what Mr. Simon says in this essay reflects his sensitivity to that contrast.

Of books on education in general and on teaching in particular there seems now to be no end. On balance, the current interest in schools is good. Those of us who have spent our lives in them are mildly exhilerated by this new

5

interest. It is comforting to have one's worries shared and a little flattering to find one's work the object of so much attention. Not that teachers are being showered with undiluted praise! Indeed, the large majority of commentators suggest (and some shout) that all is not quite well with us. It is a fact, albeit more talked about than understood, that schools and teachers do fall short of what at their best they ought to be.

But when one has brushed aside irrelevancies, penetrated thickets of clichés, and climbed over massive misconceptions, one thing about schools stands out, stark and clear. Wherever students are learning what they need and ought to know, sensing at the same time the meaning of the substance, the excitement of the process, and an irresistible urge to keep on going, at the center of the situation stands a good teacher.

Such teachers are found in many places. One may be teaching science to elementary school children, another introducing fourth graders to what they will later identify as the theory of functions. A high school instructor may be conducting an animated discussion of Shakespeare, or a Nobel Prize winner advising a graduate student on the frontiers of physics. An imaginative woman may be opening the world of poetry to the adolescents of a slum school, or a celebrated historian, backed up by a corps of technicians, may be lecturing to a television audience of millions. Whenever something of enduring value is being learned by the students who are the object of the effort, at the heart of the enterprise will be a teacher who is a master of his art.

As everyone who has ever thoughtfully attempted it will know, teaching is an art. Like other arts it can be partly explained in scientific terms but to produce it in its finest form more than science is required. Using the behavioral and social sciences as tools, it is possible to analyze the processes teachers use and to measure the responses students make. Modern technology, beginning with the printing press and including now the most advanced computers, serves the teacher in countless ways. His work, his words, his voice can be multiplied, magnified, and amplified. But the essence of teaching, the part so curiously and wonderfully compounded of knowledge, imagination, ingenuity, and empathy retains the character and the power of a high art.

Mr. Simon knows all this, for he has been a teacher. But he has the added advantage of being able to stand away from his experience far enough and long enough to view the classroom with detachment and perspective. He knows, too, that teaching calls for more than an undergraduate subject major and good intentions. He knows that even the "natural" teacher can be more effective when he prepares systematically for his work. He therefore wisely emphasizes the need for knowledge about the nature of learning and learners, about teaching techniques, about the social and philosophical concerns in which every teacher is inevitably—and should be responsibly—involved. But he also knows that success in teaching calls for a high admixture of common sense, backbone, and, not least, a lively sense of adventure.

For old-timers like me, Mr. Simon's essay is refreshing and stimulating; for beginners it offers encouragement and help; for young people wondering whether they should teach, it presents an honest and illuminating view of a profession that makes heavy demands and yields priceless rewards. For all of us, he has done a superb job.

JOHN H. FISHER

Teachers College, Columbia University
February, 1964

Contents

Preface

THIS ESSAY was written originally in 1937 in Devonshire, England, where I was enjoying a year as Exchange Professor of Education in what is now Exeter University. I had, at the time, spent ten years teaching English and music in various secondary schools and colleges in America and another five as head of the Literature Division of New College, an experimental teacher-training institution flourishing under the aegis of Columbia University's Teachers College. The following year it was published by Oxford University Press in America under the title, *Preface to Teaching*, received amiably flattering notices in the professional and lay press, went through two printings, and then went out of print.

The little book was intended as a letter of practical advice to the many aspiring teachers I had helped train by that time and to many more I had never met. An occasional letter from an unknown reader indicates that the original edition must still be available on some library shelves.

In 1940 I turned from formal teaching in academic institutions to more indirect teaching first as a music critic on a New York daily and then as a book editor. Although I have given occasional university lectures, it is more than twenty years since I have been a member in residence of any faculty.

I was therefore as apprehensive as I was flattered when Richard P. Cecil of Collier Books said he would like to bring out a paperback edition under a new title provided I would be willing to make some clearly necessary revisions. On rereading the little book after all those years, I found that I thought the general principles (particularly those developed in the final chapters, which seem to me

11

now to be the heart of the book) were still sound; and, so far as I could judge from having kept up with a good deal of reading about educational developments, so was much of the rest of it. But the great world had moved through cataclysms, and with it the educational world. Many of the specific references no longer were relevant, and some of the principles had gone along with them. Thus, in 1937 I had speculated on the effects of World War II, which was clearly on the horizon; I had delivered a polite (but I hoped devastating) attack on the thinking of a group of educators, now deceased or absorbed into other movements, known as the Frontier Thinkers; and I had offered consolation for the strong possibility—as it seemed then—that teachers stood a very good chance of never earning as much money as, say, electricians.

I have therefore gone through the original version, revising whole chapters here, substituting new examples there, bringing figures—human and statistical—up to date. Hitler is dead, and thousands of teachers earn even more than electricians do. But the basic ideas remain the same. I hope that they are sound.

HENRY W. SIMON

New York City, 1963

Chapter 1

What a Teacher Should Be Like

> Spirits that live throughout,
> Vital in every part, not as frail man,
> In entrails, heart or head, liver or veins . . .
> —MILTON
>
> The world stands out on either side
> No wider than the heart is wide;
> Above the world is stretched the sky,—
> No higher than the soul is high.
> The heart can push the sea and land
> Farther away on either hand;
> The soul can split the sky in two,
> And let the face of God shine through.
> But East and West will pinch the heart
> That cannot keep them pushed apart;
> And he whose soul is flat—the sky
> Will cave in on him by and by.
> —EDNA ST. VINCENT MILLAY

EVERYONE DOES SOME TEACHING. Parents teach their children, older children teach younger ones, experienced men teach newcomers, and friends give each other friendly advice. They are all, hopefully, imparting skill, knowledge, and insight—maybe even some wisdom—to others.

What sets the professional teacher apart, however, is precisely the fact that he is a professional. He must come to his job already equipped with a real mastery of a body of knowledge. He must find the most suitable and effective ways to train his pupils in this area of knowledge and help to develop their capacities—both intellectual and emotional—to the greatest advantage. He must do this

13

not merely through his own mastery of subjects, skills, and pedagogical "methods," but through his very character and personality. And he must be able to sustain such professional capacities throughout a long-term relationship with groups of young people.

Obviously, not everyone qualifies as a professional teacher. Simply being older than your pupils is not enough —though that was virtually the only qualification of the old village schoolmarm, who took the post because it was genteel and because there was no other way she could earn a living. It is also the only qualification of many men who drift into the profession solely because they are unfitted for the competitive world of business, and of young women who regard teaching primarily as a stop-gap between schooling and marriage.

You still hear a good deal of sentimentality about the self-sacrifice and nobility of the profession. A teacher may, of course, be self-sacrificing and noble, just as anyone else may. But such qualities are not an indispensable part of the profession, while knowledge, training, experience, and personality are. A sentimental attitude toward teaching, in fact, often leads to downright harm done boys and girls by women—and men, too—who are always wanting to mother them. Strong children resent a teacher's mothering; weak ones are made weaker by it. They usually have plenty at home. The only healthy way to regard the job is as a professional charge involving certain specific, if sometimes delicate and difficult, relationships with young human beings. To undertake the charge successfully there are three indispensable requirements, and these are:

(1) knowing at least one subject so well that you keep up an advanced study of it;

(2) knowing how to teach and train young people in that subject;

(3) having a vital pattern of life that stimulates you and, indirectly, your pupils.

I should like to make a few comments on each of these requirements.

(1) It used to be fashionable to say that the good teacher does not teach subject matter but children. This is an attractive half-truth. The whole truth, of course, is that the good teacher teaches subject matter *to* children, and therefore he must know that subject matter. Those who never study beyond a text-book, hide behind the half-truth and try to get by on the strength of a handsome smile or ingenious methods of teaching. I have seen a man—a Ph.D. in education—demonstrating how to "teach children, not subject matter" in a literature class. For a whole year he had his tenth-grade pupils happily turning over the pages of books, filling in mimeographed blanks for reports, and turning to more books. There is no doubt that the classes ran smoothly, that there was a noble array of statistics to be shown visitors, and that the teacher was a most amiable gentleman. At the end of the year he demonstrated impressively how much he had widened his class's "literary background" by publishing a monograph showing how many pages each child had read and reported on and what the names of the books were. Averages, medians, quartiles were all carefully attached. (This made his paper "scientifically" respectable.) Unfortunately, few of the books were worth reading (indeed, the teacher himself had not read many of them), and the reports contained only the titles, the authors, and three sentences of summary—mostly inaccurate. When I took charge of the class the following year, I found that even those who had "read" thirty books could not remember characters from more than two or three and that hardly anyone in the class could distinguish between a biography and a novel.

This is not an exceptional example. A tendency in the old-fashioned "progressive" schools—one that has since been widely adopted and adapted by many traditional schools—to broaden the basis of the curriculum has made hundreds try to teach what they themselves do not know. In attempts to "correlate" and "integrate" all sorts of knowledge into a single "project," you will find men and women trained in one field glibly mapping out courses in all—and "teaching" them. I have seen a young English teacher trying to lead her pupils to an understanding of the causes of the French Revolution, her own knowledge strictly confined to a reading of *A Tale of Two Cities* with notes. I have heard a former mathematics teacher make the most appalling misstatements about Mozart because he unexpectedly found himself conducting a "unit" on eighteenth century European culture. There is some excuse for these two; none for the principals who put them in charge.

But there is less than no excuse for the history teacher who can never quite remember the difference between a Jacobin and a Jacobite or the physics teacher who admits that he is rather rusty in his algebra. To teach anything you must know it well; and not only know it well, but also know its relationship to other subjects and its importance to the human race. This may seem to be a truism which scarcely needs repetition; yet Shaw's sneer that "those who can, do; those who cannot, teach" hits the mark too often to be laughed off. A good personality and a knowledge of classroom method is not enough. And, of course neither are teaching machines enough.

Still, to know your subject matter in the sense of having studied it a few years at college is not enough either. You must continue to be a student of it, always adventuring further, always finding out more. Otherwise your teaching will become dead through constant repetition. The same yellowing set of notes, the same illustrations year after year make Jack a dull boy. Probably you will not believe it, but I know a teacher who has used the same file box of classroom anecdotes for twenty years. Fortunately it gets replenished once in awhile, but the principle is wrong. Throw away your notes at least every other year and make new ones, new ones based on what you have found out about your subject meantime. "All very well," you may say, "for those who are teaching English or history, where there is constantly fresh material being made. But how about those of us who teach mathematics or elementary languages? Euclid has not appreciably altered, on the high school level, in over two thousand years, and even irregular verbs remain irregular the same way." Have you heard of semantics? have you heard of the theory of number? have you heard of the fourth dimension? And don't you even know that geometry *has* altered since Euclid—especially recently? These are subjects you may not teach your elementary pupils, but a study of them will vitalize the teaching of a language or mathematics just as surely as reading the newspaper will vitalize the teaching of history. At least, it will with a good teacher.

The least you can do is to keep up with the educational literature on your subject—the periodicals and new books that deal with the problems of teaching it. In that way you will get an occasional new idea for presenting material—not good because it is new, but good at least insofar as it is different from a way you may have been using too long. And if you have recently experimented with published "programmed" material, try throwing it away and reprogramming it yourself. It will be hard work, but it will give you a fresh slant and keep your mind alive. Also your pupils'. It is always better to keep adventuring in the subject yourself and to use your adventures in class. You can never know too much; and it is all too easy to think that you know enough. To think that is an insult to your pupils and your profession.

I am emphasizing the need for continued scholarship in the teacher partly because so many books on education tend to overlook it. You cannot get along with scholarship alone, but without it any other teaching qualifications are colorless, useless. At least, this is true in academic subjects. Administrators and athletic coaches who have not opened a book in ten years can be still quite competent; teachers of Latin, English, history, or science cannot. You can get along without theoretical training in education— many of our best teachers have done so. But you cannot make your enthusiasm for a subject contagious if that enthusiasm is so weak that you gave up learning at the end of college. In England a first class honors degree counts much more in securing a secondary school appointment than training in a school of education; and this is right, for the training necessary to attain a "first" is something in the way of guarantee that you will continue to study and that you have yourself learned how to learn. Teaching is an art with a subject matter: it is literally impossible to "teach children, not subject matter."

(2) You must also know how to teach and train young people in your chosen subject. I have said above that you can get along without theoretical training in education. This is quite true, but it is an advantage to have the training. There are other ways of acquiring it than going to lectures. One is to work for a year or two under the direct supervision of an expert teacher—the apprentice principle. Another is to learn on the job, to try various devices, methods, theories that happen to come into your head until you strike some that work. Best, of course, is to profit by all these ways—to take courses in education, work under a master, and continually experiment. You will also find that lectures on education mean much more to you after you have done some teaching. Lectures on method before teaching are something like lectures on piano-playing for a man who has never seen a keyboard: they may happen to be interesting at the time, but the very act of sitting down at the piano will drive them from his head.

To some extent your own way of learning a subject will be a guide in teaching it to children, but it is by no means always a safe guide. A common mistake of the tyro is to teach over the heads of his pupils. In my own first English class I tried to teach a group of boys and girls something of the relationship between the rhythms of poetry and of music, a subject I had recently been investigating at college. This can be taught to a high school class, as I have since found out, but not by my naïve method of lectures and readings in aesthetic theory. On the whole it is probably better to teach over the heads of children than to talk down to them: that way they at least may acquire a respect for what the subject *might* mean to them instead of a contempt for it.

But the best method is one based on a knowledge of what your pupils are really like, a knowledge that may be acquired partly through reading psychology, partly through lectures, partly through examination of their records, but above all through direct and observant contact. Thus, jazz may make a good departure for teaching about rhythms, and baseball averages good material for an arithmetic lesson; while an elementary knowledge of physiology will teach you not to lecture throughout a whole period in junior high school. Your own experiences as an adolescent learner would be a great help if you could recall them vividly enough. Most beginners think that they can, but a year or two of teaching shows them how wrong they are. Therefore it is necessary to learn from theory, from other teachers, and from trial and error.

(3) The good teacher is not merely a master of his subject and skillful in class room procedure. He is also a man, and as such influences his pupils. They may not know much about his life outside the school; but whether they do or not, it will color his relationship with them in many important ways. His attitude toward life, his way of thinking, his friendships, his prejudices, his capacity for enjoyment, his very habits of speech and dress are as inevitably a part of his teaching as any technical method. Think of the teacher who goes home each evening, marks corrections on papers that will barely be glanced at by his pupils, worries about a boy who misbehaved in class or a social slight from a local hostess, and goes to bed. He will

inevitably acquire the pedant's voice and manner and with them the pity of his contemporaries and the contempt of his classes. He should be retired at once, but he seldom is. Now think of the teacher who is not timid but curious, who takes part in local politics and is not afraid to hold his own social views, who continues to work in his own subject, to branch out into others, and to broaden his social contacts to include everyone worth including. Eventually he may be drawn from teaching into some better paid work, which is too bad. Yet he is the best teacher, the one who has most to give his pupils.

This does not mean that you should slight your teaching in order to do some vague, exciting thing called "living a full life." Rather, it means that your whole existence must make one rich pattern in which your hobbies, your home life, and your job have each a meaningful place. One can— one should—take an intelligent interest in such things as motion pictures and sports. These become sinful wastes of time only when they are indulged in with the vain hope that they may have no bearing on the rest of one's life— like secret vices. In a narrow sense, of course, you bring your outside life into the schoolroom through illustrations, even anecdotes. The man who likes sports and motion pictures and hides these facts from, say, his English class, is certainly a prig and probably a dull teacher. But in a broader and far more important sense, whatever stimulation and growth you get outside of school will make you a better teacher because it will make you a more vital person.

Yet there are two serious dangers to your chances of growing while teaching. The first is the comparative security of the profession. Once you have obtained an appointment and shown yourself reasonably competent for a beginner, you can usually hold on to it by simply behaving politely. Short of moral turpitude (or, alas, the wrong kind of political activities), there is nothing that can pry you loose from your job. Incompetence is hard to prove and no one ever thinks of discharging a teacher for stagnation. So you may fall into the easy temptation of the blameless, colorless, safe existence which most communities buy from their teachers with a sense of security.

The other danger is letting yourself be snowed under with petty administrative detail. A teacher's life is full of it, and unless he organizes work intelligently and efficiently he may spend every night reading papers and making out the many reports demanded of him. If you do that, your whole intellectual stimulus will come from your pupils as there will be time for no other. For a year or two, when you are not much older than your pupils anyway, your mind can survive; but it is a pretty sad thing to find a man of thirty-five still a high school boy intellectually. It is one way of keeping young—childish, in fact.

Here are two rules of thumb to be applied with variations:

(1) For the first six or eight years of teaching, change your post every other year—even at a financial sacrifice.

(2) Average no more than eight hours a day of *school* work throughout the school year.

Perhaps you had better not tell the interviewing officer about these rules when applying for a position.

To be something more than a cog in a wheel is, of course, your duty to your pupils. But once you regard it as that, you are already lost. The teacher who visits a picture gallery or reads a book because he thinks he ought to do it for the sake of the little ones, might almost as well not do it at all. Your first duty is to yourself. Children instinctively react to vitality and will get its full benefit soon enough. The teacher who "puts everything he has into his job" is really not worth very much if there isn't much to put. Better a first-rater who gives only half of himself than a third-rater who gives all. Best is having all of a first-rater.

In this respect a teacher is like a poet or a minister.

Nothing that he does is alien to his job. A business man, so long as he is efficient in business hours, can usually spend the rest of his time as he likes—in creative activity or puerilities. Either may be equally unrelated to his business. But everything a teacher does bears a relationship to his teaching. It may be a good or a bad relationship, but eventually it will show. As with the poet and the minister, the teacher's job draws on all of him, and the first-rate teacher has a large amount to draw on. In the last analysis, then, your job is to be first-rate.

Chapter 2

What the Teacher Can Do for the Individual

> But yield who will to their separation,
> My object in living is to unite
> My avocation and my vocation
> As my two eyes make one in sight.
> Only where love and need are one,
> And the work is play for mortal stakes,
> Is the deed ever really done
> For Heaven and the future's sakes.
> —ROBERT FROST

BECAUSE THE WORLD has grown infinitely smaller during the past fifty years, and done so at an accelerating rate; because the hot and cold wars, the arms race, the economic and military power clusters, the growth of power in government, business, and labor have made it almost impossible for anyone to be strictly a private citizen and have made all of us far more mutually dependent than ever before, the trend in education has been, in our lifetime, toward dealing with "practical" problems.

Science, at about the turn of the century, began to compete with the humanities as a field of specialization in colleges. In the thirties, it was social science that began to compete both with humanities and with natural science. Now, in competition with the U.S.S.R., natural science has sputniked ahead, not only on the college level but all the way down to the elementary level, and the humanities and arts are having to fight harder than ever for serious attention—and appropriations. The subject of education, in the meantime, has been trying to take on the character of both pure science and natural science, and we tend to forget that in the quaint old days when the subject of education was called "pedagogy," it was regarded primarily as an art. It is, of course, none of these things—or, rather, something of each. Each phase that education has passed through has broadened its scope and taught us new ways of looking at it; but the danger now is that in considering the social implications of the subject we may forget most of what we have learned before.

One thing that tends to be thrown overboard is our cultural heritage. In a vain attempt to earn the consideration of apostles of "the useful" in education, classics teachers once tried to prove that training in dead languages is a "mental discipline." Geometrists frequently have been driven to the same pathetic position, and now teachers of literature, wishing to hang on to a course that will include their beloved Milton and Shakespeare, are also on the defensive.

If you are a teacher of one of these "useless" subjects, do not put yourself into the hopeless position of justifying your existence by trying to prove that your enthusiasms will be profitable acquisitions to the student who wants to be sure of a job when he leaves school—a job and nothing more. You cannot compete on those grounds either with the health director or the teacher of stenography and "business English." Nor should you try to show (even though you might be able to succeed) that boys who know Euclid, Virgil, Shakespeare, and Bach have been on the whole more public-minded *and* comfortably off than those who do not. Such arguments are based on a false assumption: that all education has the sole purpose of making boys and girls more economically or socially useful.

The purpose of purely cultural studies lies rather in the studies themselves, in the value they have for the individual, not for society. The man who truly studies Plato or Beethoven is different forever after—I had almost said "better," but that would be begging the question. The value in cultural studies is not measurable, but it is easily demonstrable. Consider the two or three most cultured men and women you know, and then try to imagine what they would be like without their study of philosophy, literature, the arts, or "pure" science (i.e., useless science). It is all but impossible to imagine them without their cultural backgrounds, as profound study in such subjects makes a human being profoundly different. Consider now the stenographer without her shorthand and typing skills or even the dentist without his skill in filling teeth. Though you would not employ them, they would still be essentially the same human beings. The merely useful may at any time be discarded and the person will not be essentially changed. A knowledge of our cultural heritage may in part be forgotten; it can never be discarded. Its value, as I said, cannot be measured, but you might try asking a cultivated man what his background is worth to him. It would be an idiotic question, but his explanation of that fact would show you why commercial or social education cannot be evaluated in the same terms as cultural.

I am not trying to argue for cultural education at the expense of useful. As a matter of fact, in many classes the two are practically indistinguishable,—or should be, as I shall try later to show. What I am trying to argue is that social and commercial use are not the only criteria by which to judge. The very developments in our economic and social world show us how true this is. More and more, people are being relieved of day-long routine work. Only a little over a century ago Robert Owen was considered a fool if not a dangerous radical for reducing working hours in his factory from seventeen to ten a day. Now we are down to a forty-four hours week, forty, thirty-six—it may be twenty-four by the time you read this. One of the problems of the teacher is to train his pupils in a worthy use for all these liberated hours.

Now, in times of prosperity, the answer that Americans have found to this problem is to add to an already large list of subjects certain others that are supposed to afford "education for leisure." The underlying assumption is that every boy and girl should be prepared for the grim business of earning a living and the vaguer one of being a good citizen; then, if time and money permit, he may also receive some training in "frills" such as music, art, and the drama. The "frills" are regarded as "cultural," the rest as the serious business of education. Shortly after a depression comes to town, however, the frills are cut off and the rest allowed to remain, possibly with a reduced staff. Such a policy is regarded as "sensible"; schooling may be a little less attractive than it was, but the essential job is being done. "If the three r's were good enough for Abe Lincoln, they ought to be good enough for anyone." So runs the argument.

Such an attitude is ludicrously wrong. It assumes that certain subjects are cultural and therefore easily dispensed with, while others are training in the real business of life. *All* subjects (with the exception of a few strictly skill subjects like stenography) are cultural subjects, or would be if they were properly taught and learned. The result of regarding culture as a frill in life is seen in the way we Americans use our leisure. The popularity of our Disneylands and the hollowness of the large majority of our television programs testify to a profound national conviction that anything artistic or any art that takes life seriously is "high brow"—therefore a bore, therefore a frill. Our leisure is spent escaping from ourselves. Once the serious business of the day is over (that is, making money or running a house), we strenuously dash away from ourselves, usually in a closed car to be sure to keep nature out. The amusements we have developed more than any other country are motion pictures, automobiles, and television—all as means of escape.

It would be an exaggeration to lay the whole blame on our schools. Yet the school both reflects and aids this national attitude in measuring the value of its offerings entirely by their external usefulness. No wonder music and the other arts are regarded as trimmings; no wonder (and this is much worse) arithmetic, geography, and the languages are regarded as things to be "passed"—that is, to be got over with and remembered only when there is a practical use for them. Your job, if you teach any subject that is less obviously "cultural" than music or the fine arts, is to make of it too a truly cultural subject. That means that you must develop your pupils fundamentally, must make of them fuller, richer persons mentally, physically, or morally, must develop their awareness of things, their understandings, and their powers of appreciation and expression. Any teaching which does not get under the pupils' skins and make them eventually different and better persons might almost as well not take place at all. The training they get from you should be apparent in the way they spend their leisure; but it should also affect the way they regard their jobs and the way they work in them.

Your teaching of arithmetic, for example, may merely train your class in a number of processes which will let them pass an examination at the end of the term. That is "useful." It may also help them manage their savings accounts better or get a job on graduation. That is useful too—and this time without quotation marks. But if you can develop in them an understanding of number relations, if you can teach them to visualize distances and quantities, to appreciate imaginatively the meaning of "ten million" or of "one thousandth of an inch," then you are training them culturally: they will forever after be more sensitive, more appreciative, more understanding, even though they may do no better on a formal examination.

It may be objected that if we made all our boys and girls cultured human beings, if we succeeded in training them to be sensitive to the arts and the life about them and to have some sort of philosophical insight into the implications of nature, science, and society, we would be miseducating them for much of the necessary work of the world. That is, so long as there are floors to be scrubbed and simple routinized processes in factories and on farms, it would be a mistake to raise the level of culture among the masses of the population; we should merely be making them unhappy, and incidentally inefficient, in the jobs they have to do.

There are two answers to this objection. The first is that we are so far from being in any such danger now, and the business of raising the level of culture of a nation is so slow and difficult, that we really need not worry for many a generation—maybe centuries—to come. The other answer is that any such objection implies a profound misunderstanding of the meaning of "culture." It implies a distinction between work and leisure that ought not to exist. A cultured person is not one who, having a certain amount of leisure, devotes it to the fine arts but does not let such interests enter the working part of his life. Rather he is one whose whole pattern of life is affected by his knowledge of Palestrina and Leonardo da Vinci. Beauty and truth to him lie in steel or in the passing of the seasons on his farm, in the maturing of his children and his relationships with his fellow workmen. The man with a mature sense of values, one based on a sensitive appreciation of the world about him, needs no roller coaster or Brigitte Bardot to make him forget his own insignificance. He senses and accepts his relationship to the world about him. He is the truly cultured man.

Do not make the mistake, as many do, of thinking that

by developing a boy's capacity to appreciate cultural subjects and thus making him a cultured man, you are educating him for "happiness." Of course, there is happiness and contentment to be found in music, literature, philosophy, history, art, and science. But to develop certain sensitivities to art, the capacity for moral questioning, and the critical and sceptical approach of science is potentially to open the door for your pupils to huge vistas of discontent and unhappiness. Through such education you are making him more peculiarly a man than he would otherwise have been, and man is natural heir to many sharp, subtle miseries and sorrows that a cow may never aspire to. But neither may she aspire to the heights.

To develop cultured individuals is part of the job of the teacher. It means hard work both for himself and for his pupils; for it means acquiring the heritage of our culture, and without hard work it can never be earned. You may through various classroom techniques and circus-like stunts be able to keep up an interest in your pupils while you are with them; but until that interest is so much a part of them that they will continue work in the subject year after year, until formulae, irregular verbs, or natural laws represent indispensable tools for something far more important than examinations to be passed or games to be played, your subject matter has no real cultural value for them—it is not a part of them. And until you have at least helped in developing a cultured human being, you have never taught—you have only "kept school."

Chapter 3

Why the Teacher Cannot Reform the World

> The king can drink the best of wine—
> > So can I;
> And has enough when he would dine—
> > So have I;
> And cannot order rain or shine—
> > Nor can I.
> Then where's the difference—let me see—
> Betwixt my lord the king and me?
> > —CHARLES MACKAY

IT SEEMS IMPOSSIBLE that you should be alive, young, and a teacher in our troubled times without having some social and political convictions, and that these convictions should not appear important to you. For no matter what you teach—even if it is music or needlework—social and political issues are in some way going to enter your teaching life. The very fact that you are an employee of the state or of private employers makes this inevitable; and you may as well take stock of what you can and cannot do about your convictions in the role of teacher.

Let us then see what sort of thing a school is. It is first of all an agent of the state entrusted with the training of the young. In pre-literate societies this training goes on at home. When society is so simple that the training consists only in hunting and fighting or in very simple housekeeping and crop-raising, no special educational institution is needed. Parents and other relatives can very well take care of this teaching while doing the jobs themselves, incidentally training the young in the manners and morals of the tribe. There may be special occasional ceremonies at adolescence or marriage, but the whole business is simple and direct.

When, however, society becomes more complex, when it requires of its young such complicated skills as reading and writing or a more advanced method of warfare—skills which not every adult in the community himself possesses —it is necessary to engage a schoolmaster and to set up the institution of the school. The training in skills passes out of the hands of the family, and with it passes some of the education in emotions and attitudes. Society always has been careful to see to it that the schoolmaster educates for emotions and attitudes which it approves of. The school in this sense remains always an agent of society. This is a simple and important fact to keep in mind. You will sometimes find it extremely difficult to keep it there, because you will wish it weren't so. I am not even saying that it ought to be so; but it is, and you cannot alter a fact by wishing it different.

Now, in the primitive society the training is not only simple and direct; it is also highly effective. In fact, you will usually find that the more simple and direct an education is, the more effective it is too—not necessarily the better, but, I repeat, the more effective. When society knows exactly what it wants of its young, when what it wants is nothing more than a few easily acquired skills and a few simple, strong emotions, and when that training is given almost twenty-four hours a day by adults who themselves profoundly possess these skills and emotions, the young will also acquire these skills quickly and well. They will have no concepts other than those that are repeatedly given them: they will be narrowly but effectively trained. Generally speaking, then, the simpler the objective, the more effective the training.

This easily understood principle also holds in a society that is more complex than the tribal, but now it acquires one important corollary. That is—if a simple objective is to remain simple, it must be clearly understood by everyone and accepted as well. There must be no powerful groups within the society who disagree, who think that the young should be trained for something entirely different. Such a group inevitably complicates matters so much that neither its own objectives nor those of the majority can be as effectively attained as if the group did not exist. The resulting education may be in many respects better—it will almost certainly be broader—but it cannot be so effective. That is why a totalitarian state is likely to have a more effective education than a democracy.

One historical example will make my meaning quite clear. In the Sparta of the eleventh century B.C. the ratio of slaves to citizens was about five to one, and Sparta was surrounded by other city-states, mostly hostile. The one purpose of her rulers therefore was to preserve her from potential internal and external enemies. Accordingly, the Spartan boy was taken from his mother at the age of seven and put into a military camp, his father probably being away at another. There the boy stayed, excepting when he was on campaigns, till the age of thirty. For the whole twenty-three years he was under strict military discipline and trained in the skills and virtues of soldiering. He learned to obey, to fight; never to flee, never to give quarter, never to think. Sparta survived all dangers for several hundred years: there has probably never been so effective an educational system.

But in order to achieve any such effectiveness, the state must first of all have a clearly defined objective, like Sparta's, and secondly its government must be absolute. The country that adopts the objective must agree with the Fascist, the Nazi, and the Communist social tenet—that the individual exists for the state, not the state for the individual. Neither of these conditions can a modern democracy readily achieve, except to a limited degree in times of national catastrophe (when the nation relinquishes some of its democratic character and processes) or as a reaction to a national shock. Thus, in wartime the training and education given to the millions of members of the armed forces has clear, simple objectives and is given by an absolute authority. It can be, thus, as direct and effective as the training given to all children, even in peace-time, in a monolithic, totalitarian state.

Again, we have seen a limited manifestation of this principle in our country when the shock of the first sputnik of the U.S.S.R. inspired a sharp stepping up of our pro-gram of training in the physical sciences in every part of the country and on every level of education from the elementary through graduate school. But this stepping up could never be so effective and efficient as in a nation whose central government decrees that it will train thou-sands of scientists in a number of fields and dictates pre-cisely who should be given this training, how many years and how may hours a day should be given to it, and exactly what the training should consist of.

Excepting, then, within the armed forces, a modern democracy cannot have clearly defined, simple educa-tional objectives and achieve them through a centrally conceived and unobstructed program financed and admin-istered by a central government. The reason it cannot lies in its very nature. For democracy is a group of persons or peoples that governs itself, that lives under laws it makes for itself, and that retains the supreme power of changing those laws when it wants to. It assumes the justice of the principle of government by the will of the majority; and that very fact postulates the existence of a minority or minorities. Where minorities exist, there is always a dif-ference of opinion, and where there is a difference of opinion, objectives can never be so clearly and finally defined as where there is not. It is the virtue of democracy that it thrives on difference of opinion, that it harbors free speech, and that it tries to make use of the best it can find, giving one party platform a chance when another has failed. A totalitarian state, like Sparta, assumes that it has found the truth and will tolerate no dissenting ideas, let alone actions. It is, therefore, much easier to define the educational objectives of Germany under the Nazis or of the U.S.S.R. under the Communist Party than of democratic England or the United States. It is easier to attain an effective education for a country that knows just where it wants to go than for one that is not quite so sure. Remember those four words—"not quite so sure."

The natural inference from this might be that a teacher should therefore always teach just what he thinks is right, and that by so doing he will contribute to that healthy difference of opinions from which a democracy evolves its destiny. I wish this were so. If it were, teachers might be a great deal more honest and wholehearted, particularly in dealing with current social problems, than they can now often afford to be. But if you think it is so, then you have forgotten the principle I told you was very difficult to keep in mind—that the school is the agent of the state.

For though a modern democracy tolerates and even encourages a certain amount of difference of opinion on most matters, it stops far short of the logical conclusion which would be anarchy. The democracy is only "not *quite* so sure" as the totalitarian state about certain very important ideas. Democracy will, for instance, be more tolerant of conflicting views on labor, sex, and taxation than will a totalitarian state, but it will seldom tolerate extreme views on any of these subjects. When it comes to government, democracy is still more strict in what it will not tolerate: it will, for example, not tolerate its own overthrow in favor of totalitarianism.

This comparative narrowness is accentuated in the schools of a democracy, for schools always have been and probably always will be comparatively late expressions of the society that creates them as an instrument. Because a school is a complex and difficult thing to create, it is almost always behind the more advanced thinking of the society. There is in the school a natural "cultural lag" simply because a state must first decide approximately what it wants its schools to do and then find means for having them do it. This takes time. A school is a powerful and strongly forged instrument designed by the state to carry out its own designs; it is not a proper, or even a good, tool for altering those designs.

This natural conservatism of the school, this cultural lag, was eloquently recognized by the U. S. Supreme Court when, in 1955, it decreed integration in the schools of the country but ruled that it should be achieved "with all deliberate speed." But the eloquence became figurative stammering when certain Southern states put up "massive resistance" and achieved token—if any—integration with *un*due deliberateness, and then only, in two instances, with the advent of armed force and bloodshed.

In politics, in industry, in law, even in housing, Negroes had made significant if not spectacular advances before the intervention of the Supreme Court's decision on schools, while in the armed forces (by nature the most absolutist aspect of our national life) real progress was made with a stroke of President Eisenhower's pen. However, progress in the schools lags behind not only in the South but in many parts of the country.

Schools, one is tempted to conclude on the basis of this, are reactionary and are obstacles to social progress, and conservative and reactionary elements in any community will use violence to keep them so. Socrates tried teaching unconventional ideas, and his reward was a cup of hemlock. In our own times, a distressingly large number of college professors have found themselves out of jobs on account of their unconventional opinions. The relevant fact about such case histories is that even when the victim's ideas have triumphed in the end—or at least achieved wide acceptance—they have not done so first within the schools. The body politic must first accept an idea, and only after it has lived with it for a while in peace can it tolerate its dissemination to the young.

A generation ago, before World War II, there was a

group of professors of education, scattered among various institutions, called the "social frontier thinkers." They examined society and saw that everything wasn't wonderful. Something ought to be done, they laudably decided, and they chose, of all things, the schools to do it with. That was, of course, the most handy tool for them to choose, one they knew a good deal about, but it was not adapted to their purpose. As long as they had confined their teachings to lectures and writings in "educational philosophy," as long as their ideas were expressed in the conventional gobbledygook of professional journals addressed to each other, no one paid much attention. But when they ventured on mildly left-wing interpretations of history in textbooks to be read by children, an outcry was heard throughout the land, boards of education (seldom graced with the presence of a professional educator) denounced them and threw out their books, and within a few years all was again conservatively quiet along the Potomac and all points North, South and West.

So if you are out to advocate communism, free love, the principles of the John Birch Society, the single tax, or any other radical social philosophy in your teaching, don't try to gain your ends through the schools, for you can't. You can't, because the way to achieve Communism or Fascism is not to lay a hand on one of the tools of the state—the school—but to seize the very state itself.

First the state, then the school, has always been the order of fundamental change. Even in Sparta, Lycurgus developed his school system only two hundred years after the state itself had taken definite form. It might be a fine thing if we could achieve a peaceful revolution for social or political justice by teaching our children to have different concepts of property or class distinction or racial purity from those dominant in our society. But before you are allowed to do that, you must get the state to give you permission; you must persuade it that your particular social philosophy is the only correct one. And states seldom let themselves be persuaded to accept a new order without the use of machine guns.

Nor can you get anywhere simply by calling your ideas "an educational philosophy," as the frontier thinkers first tried to do. For the fact is that any significant educational philosophy is necessarily the expression of a social philosophy. The dominant—that is, working—educational philosophy of America today is quite as complicated and amorphous an outgrowth of a vaguely understood "American democracy" as is our social philosophy. America's faith in local government and in giving every individual an equal chance receives lip service in both our educational and our *de facto* social philosophy; and the application of that faith is almost as erratic and whimsical in schools as it is in society at large. Schools follow the rest of society in these and in other matters. They cannot lead.

Even our most advanced schools are only late reflections of what the more advanced thinkers have been saying for some time. Recent liberalization in sex education and in relations between pupils and teachers could never have occurred if they had not been preceded by a break-down of old-fashioned sexual morality and respect for elders. The most a school can hope to do is to train in that aspect of social philosophy which it considers best and which *will be tolerated by the existing society*. Even this may take great courage.

If, then, you are out to reform the world, if you are a social revolutionary, do not try to effect your work through the schools. Be a real revolutionary and organize revolutionary cells or platoons of colored shirts. You can even organize propaganda rallies and—as certain reactionary crackpots do now—misname them "schools." After you have effected your revolution, then start paying attention to the real schools, raising the next generation to think and feel as you do—or at least as you want it to.

But if you still insist on becoming a teacher and still insist on living up even to your unorthodox social opinions,

I think I can tell you just how far you can go in the classroom with them. You can go with them just up to the point where you are taken seriously, but no further. So long as you are considered only "young," "interesting," "promising," our democratic tradition of free speech will let you have a large amount of scope in many localities. But just as soon as you achieve the epithet "dangerous," that is, just as soon as you are starting to become effective, out you go. You will then be in the excellent company of Socrates.

Chapter 4

What the Teacher Can Do for Society

Patriotism has become a mere national self-assertion, a sentimentality of flag-cheering with no constructive duties.

—H. G. WELLS

I HOPE that it is now clear why the teacher cannot decide on some solution for the troubles of the world and, by teaching it in school, bring about a millennium or even a pretty mild improvement on the muddle we are generally in. It is not his job to do so any more than it is the physician's or the baker's. But it is part of the teacher's job to help train his pupils in those qualities of mind and character, those abilities and attitudes, that can be useful in coping with whatever muddle the future may hold for them. What that particular muddle will be, the teacher is not called upon to decide. If political economists and sociologists disagree as eloquently as they do, a group of amateurs like the staff of a school is arrogantly foolish to try to do better. All that may reasonably be expected of a teacher is to realize that the world will be an appreciably different world ten years from now, that superficial sets of loyalties and values will be a handicap to improvement, and that certain qualities like moral courage, clarity of thought, and adaptability may be a help in grappling with social problems.

Such education is called "training for citizenship." It used to be (and still is in our more benighted schools) simply a matter of making hundred per cent patriots of all the little boys and girls—a salute to the flag each morning, memorizing the "Star Spangled Banner," and history texts that stressed the bloodier military victories. The objective was an unquestioning my-country-right-or-wrong attitude—a good one only for soldiers in trenches. Totalitarian states achieve this objective much more effectively with powerful tools learned from modern psychology— uniforms, marching, youth camps, and the worship of living instead of dead "heroes."

Although a modern democracy should be made up of citizens who have a good idea as to what democracy is, who know how to think and act, and are not blindly led by a man who represents bread and circuses and who periodically rattles a sword or an atomic bomb to whip up "patriotism."

The job in the totalitarian state is comparatively easy. It is comparatively easy to teach a vast majority of the population *not* to think, and to react with violent emotions to such concepts as "imperialist," "foreigner," "Wall Street," "Jew," "foreigner," "bourgeois," or "our glorious history." It is infinitely harder to teach people to see more sides to a question than one, to weigh justice, to make intelligent sacrifices, and to act with firm discretion.

I do not want here to discuss the comparative merits of different types of states, but it is pertinent to repeat that effective education is harder to achieve in a democracy than in a totalitarian state because the democracy aims higher. The success of a totalitarian government depends upon the development of the herd instinct and animal savagery; the success of a democracy depends upon an enlightened citizenry capable of reasonable and harmonious action; that is, it depends on the development of the highest, least animal-like characteristics of which man is capable.

Such characteristics include clarity of thought, intellectual and emotional honesty, the ability to lead and to follow both intelligently and effectively, and the willingness to make personal sacrifices for the good of the state. These are not abstractions which may be developed in a vacuum; nor are they frameless qualities, like physical strength, that can be used for any appropriate job. Rather, they are skills, habits, and attitudes which must be developed in more or less specific situations if they are to be at all effective. And they are not easy to develop.

Let us analyse what it means to train one of these qualities—clarity of thought—in a citizen. Teaching the habit of thinking carefully and soundly in almost any given situation is difficult first of all because thinking is one of the least loved of all occupations, and because precision in thought is almost the last thing a child is willing to learn. You can make a class practically perfect in a mathematical process like factoring, but you can never reach anything like perfection with original problems because they require thought.

An assignment in an English class to write a composition is usually done with dutiful acquiescence, for after all a large part of the time required is occupied with the more or less mechanical processes of forming letters, spelling, and punctuation. Give, however, a series of assignments in outlining ideas for compositions, and you will be considered a harsh master. Such assignments are—or should be—almost pure thinking. Few can stand much of that.

A second difficulty encountered in training for clear thinking is the really hard job of teaching the necessary skills with language. Most thinking that is not day-dreaming is done with language symbols—words, sentences, and paragraphs—and precision is needed to make the thinking effective. Usually a faculty likes to leave this training to the English teachers partly because it requires detailed, continuous routine, like acquiring skill on the piano, and partly because most teachers of other subjects do not know the difference between precise and unprecise English. The result is that English exercises may show precision in the use of language while papers written for history or economics classes, or even exercises in translation from a foreign language, fall way below an acceptable standard. You cannot expect a consistent habit to grow by training it, say, from nine to ten each day and disregarding it from ten to three.

English teachers themselves do none too well. Mistaken ideas of "appreciation," "self-expression," and "creative writing" tend nowadays to get in the way of clear understanding and precise writing. The French do better. Through their devices of *explication de texte*, word-study, and careful preparation and revision of essays from the elementary school up, they have made of themselves a nation of clear thinkers and clear speakers. I am not referring only to university graduates and members of the Academie: almost any French cab driver or shopgirl who has left school at the age of twelve will illustrate my point.

Practically from the time he first learns to handle the alphabet, he is trained rigorously in grammar, in the development of an idea in a paragraph, in the denotation and connotation of every word. Then he is taught to model his own use of language on that of the most brilliant stylists in French literature.

Read sometimes Rollo Brown's *How the French Boy Learns to Write* and you will understand how a nation of clear thinkers is developed. In point of clarity the French press leaves the American and English stumbling far behind in a muddle of ill-digested verbiage. If our English teachers could begin to approach the precision of the work of the French and if they could make their colleagues cooperate, a step forward would be taken in training for citizenship.

Not that I would recommend following the French system slavishly. Its chief shortcoming, from the point of view of training citizens, is that its study of literature is confined almost entirely to the classics, and its composition exercises are too often essays in abstractions. The citizen of a democracy needs not only the tools and skills for clear thinking; he also needs to practise these skills on pertinent questions. And abstracted clarity of language has scarcely been enough to help the French nation avoid disastrous political chaos. Training in geometry or Latin may teach you to think clearly in Euclid and Caesar but not in deciding how to vote.

Enter here our third difficulty. In our social sciences especially, it is extremely hard, for reasons mentioned in the previous chapter, to teach an honest citizenship based on a consideration of all the facts. Some teachers may tell the true story of the Hayes-Tilden election scandal so far as it is known. Few have either permission or courage to tell about diplomatic lying in our own recent history; and practically none dares mention scandal in local politics. In civics courses pupils learn how many congressmen there are, who elects them, and how voting machines are operated; but they do not often learn the less savory aspects of raising party funds or what deals are made in hotel rooms at party conventions. You may teach pupils to think clearly and act honestly about the law of the lever, or about the plays of Richard Sheridan, but not about some of the forces that profoundly affect them as citizens.

I am not advocating a course in scandalmongering; nor would I like to see classical literature and mathematics left out of our schools. What I should like is to see our boys and girls receiving rigid training in the use of the tools of clear thinking—that is, in language—and to exercise these tools on realistic problems of citizenship in a modern democracy, with a fearless presentation of fact. This might result in an enlightened citizenry trained to think clearly.

One of the reasons for reading Caesar, Shakespeare, Milton, and Burke is to gain a control of language. I should like to see our teachers consciously turn the controls they are teaching through the classics to a criticism of the daily newspapers and to contemporary novels, plays, motion pictures, and television shows that deal with social issues. It is true that we are way ahead of the French in using contemporary literature, but we tend to avoid all controversial issues.

Should you try a program that included rigid training in language skills and realistic discussion of modern authors who deal with controversial issues, you would very shortly come against the last and most serious obstacle to clear thinking—emotion.

If the issues brought up in discussion are really vital to the pupils, that is, if the clarity of thought is to be really tested in a laboratory that means something, then emotion is bound to color the thinking of practically everyone present. The test for your training—ultimately the test for democracy—will lie in the ability shown by the group to respect fact, to weigh dispassionately, to use precise language—in short, to think clearly on matters of civic importance.

It should now be unnecessary to warn you that such courageous and important teaching as this is dangerous: parents and school officials are likely to feel even more strongly than your pupils on the issues raised, false reports will start flying round, and shortly you will be in trouble. If you have been preaching to your pupils instead of judiciously having all sides to a question examined, then you will deserve your trouble. But if you have been scrupulously impartial and have protected yourself by keeping careful records, you may in many communities wave the banner of free speech and do much good with your work. Some trouble there is almost bound to be, but it is the sort of trouble I should advise you to court rather than avoid. No man was ever worth anything who did not make enemies, and too few teachers have them.

From this brief analysis of what it means to teach clarity of thought to citizens, it is obvious that the intellect is not all that needs to be trained. One needs to find citizen-like situations in which to exercise the clarity, and one needs to train the emotions as well. With the less intellectual qualities of the good citizen—like cooperativeness or ability to work with others, willingness to identify one's own interests with those of a group, responsibility, courage, and honesty—the exercise in real situations is even more important. The old-fashioned schoolmaster was all too prone to think a boy showed the qualities of a good citizen if he never cheated in his home-work (honesty), was willing to help clean the blackboards or take care of younger boys (cooperativeness), and stood punishment in the classroom or on the football field without wincing (courage). Such qualities are all well and good: we should rather have our boys with than without them. Yet they give no real promise that the pupils will make good citizens. Academic honesty and financial honesty are really two quite different things. A boy may be able to "cooperate" beautifully with his teacher by always taking orders perfectly but may be totally useless in the more citizen-like situation of getting on with his equals. A man may be a perfect sport on the playing field and a perfect mucker in business. He may be courageous before an onrushing bull and afraid to look a social issue in the face. It is therefore necessary to encourage those types of extracurricular activities which will develop the most desirable qualities for the citizen of a democracy. A strong self-government organization, for example, will be more useful for this purpose than a well coached football team, and a set of elected class officers will serve the purpose better than monitors or prefects handpicked by a teacher.

To give these qualities their sturdiest exercise, the teacher should always remain in the background as much as possible. The school principal or the faculty adviser who insists on okaying every expenditure of the dramatic club weakens seriously the value of the training a pupil treasurer can get. Let your pupils make errors, even bad errors. Without them they will never learn what will work or who will work. The weak reliance that results from close supervision may set a ready stage for any potential dictator with a plausible quack panacea.

This, then, is what the teacher can do about reforming the world. He cannot preach his chosen way to salvation, but he can develop qualities in his pupils that may help them find their own. If this sounds too slow and indirect for your temperament, teaching is probably not your job.

Chapter 5

How Not to Be a Schoolmarm

The sallow, virgin-minded, studious
Martyr to mild enthusiasm.
—BROWNING
The wretched souls of those who lived
Without or praise or blame, with that ill band
Of angels mix'd, who nor rebellious proved
Nor yet were true to God.
—DANTE
Much have I seen and known,—cities of men,
And manners, climates, councils, governments,
Myself not least, but honoured of them all,—
And drunk delight of battle with my peers,
Far on the ringing plains of windy Troy.
I am a part of all that I have met . . .
—TENNYSON

THE "TYPICAL" representative of a profession is seldom a distinguished member of it. There is the type of man you would classify on sight as "lawyer"—but not Abraham

Lincoln, Francis Bacon, or Franklin Roosevelt. Such men are too broad in outlook and in background to fit readily into any type. So was John Dewey. So was Socrates.

The typical school-teacher—the schoolmarm of either sex—is something no one wants to be. His characteristics, almost the opposite of those I described in Chapter 1, are timidity, a peculiar refinement or super-gentility, and an overconscientiousness about trivialities. Such a man or woman cannot be a good teacher because he cannot be a leader. Yet it is difficult to avoid acquiring these characteristics: they are thrust upon one partly by the nature of school life but even more by public opinion.

A teacher's life is, in a small town, practically public property: almost everyone regards himself as a duly constituted censor of a teacher's behavior—not to mention his professional skill, though that does not concern us here. Your physician may play poker if he wants to and your chauffeur get drunk on his nights off; but in many places the teacher dare not do the first and almost nowhere dare he do the second. He is expected to live up to the standards that parents and school boards preach, let them practise what they will. The board is composed usually of a community's most respected citizens, and it sees to it that the teachers exhibit the virtues for which the board is respected.

The underlying principle is sound enough. If the school is an agent of the state (see Chapter 3) and if a teacher's whole life affects his teaching (see Chapter 1), then it is up to the school board to see to it that the teacher leads a desirable life. The difficulty and the injustice comes in the narrow interpretation given by most school boards to the phrase "desirable life." It is too likely to be based on superficial convention and desk-motto philosophy.

In small towns particularly, the teacher thus becomes not a courageous, independent thinker and an adventuresome person, as the leader of children ought to be, but a timid soul censored by a board and spied upon by everyone. Consideration of his every action is prefaced by those two hamstringing words, *"Dare I?"* "Dare I wear these clothes?" "Dare I go to this restaurant?" "Dare I be seen soon again with this young man or woman?" "Dare I vote thus?" "Dare I say this?" And finally, "Dare I think so-and-so?" He must attend certain functions and not others, live in a certain district, and maintain a certain standard of living even though his salary may not justify it. The result is almost inevitably a timidity and conservatism dictated not by conviction but by social pressure. So long as he does and says only what the most staid, respectable, and conservative members of the community do and say, he is safe; so long as he thinks no thoughts that cannot be uttered in the presence of the tenderest girl in school, his job is secure. Beyond this there may lie danger—a danger he should be ready to welcome.

This picture is extreme but not exaggerated. Some places permit more growth and freedom than others, but the principle is the same. He is permitted far more latitude in a New York high school than in a Kentucky mountain district, but so is everyone else. Where everyone has great latitude, he is given some; where everyone has some, he has little; where everyone has little, he has none.

It would be almost as foolish to argue with this state of affairs as to argue with a law of nature. With possibly the single exception of Mexico, where economic and political control are not closely identified with each other, a people gets the sort of education its controlling group wants it to have. In the United States, where there is more local option in education than in any other great western country, local prejudices are sure to affect the teacher intimately. And local prejudices will as a rule tend to make a schoolmarm of a teacher.

You cannot, as I said, argue with the general principle; but you can, if you are courageous, do something about the force of local prejudices. You can make a community allow you to think and act as a self-respecting man or woman should. You have to bow to the law of society that a people gets the sort of education its controlling group wants, but you can also do something toward making it want a better sort—the sort that is given by one who is not only a leader of children but a leader of men as well. Only when the teacher himself becomes a force in the community, only when he has earned the respect of the adults among whom he lives, can he become a genuine force in education. From Socrates and Jesus down, occasional teachers have earned the serious consideration of their communities in varying degrees. So far as I know, no American teachers have ever achieved a cup of hemlock or a cross while fighting for consideration, nor have they encountered shotguns or concentration camps as some Mexican and German teachers did in the early 1930's. Our opponents have been only Mrs. Grundys and narrow-minded legislators, our punishments gossip, or, at worst, dismissal.

But one must not underestimate the difficulties that can be put in the way of a teacher who wishes to become a leader in the community. The first and most obvious one I have mentioned already—the strait-laced ideas and conduct that are sometimes demanded. The easy course is to knuckle under, get used to it, and lead a dull, respectable life forever after. There is nothing inherently wrong about respectability so long as one does not assume that cloistered virtue for fear of developing more vigorous ones. But unquestioning acceptance of *any* set of values is deadening and makes bad teachers.

The opposite course is to kick over the traces, to flaunt an independence of gossip, or, to call it by a more polite name, public opinion. This is equally unwise because it readily leads to quixoticism. If local prejudice demands that you give up cards or smoking or certain restaurants, you had better not make an issue of the matter before you are firmly established. Such deprivations are superficial and essentially unimportant even though they may be highly annoying. There is no sense in rubbing a community of Mrs. Grundys the wrong way on precisely those matters which appear the most important to them but which are in reality only symbols.

Give them victory with symbols every time: that will only strengthen your position when it comes to something important. The issue worth fighting for will come soon enough, and you can recognize it by knowing that it involves principles much more far-reaching than your personal convenience. Such an issue may be professional and involve the question of whether or not you give true historical interpretations or only sugar-coated half-truths. It may, on the other hand, be personal, and involve the question of whom you marry or even, if you are a girl, whether you may marry at all. The teacher who has not flaunted his disrespect for the conventions of his community in regard to symbols is in a far better position to fight his real battles. "We might have known—" will be the attitude of the school board whose new appointee wore a low-cut dress one week and mentioned Karl Marx the next. If she could have earned the reaction expressed in the words "Such a fine person—maybe there's something in it," she might have taken a first step toward academic freedom.

Give in on little issues with grace even if you cannot do it with conviction. Then you may be able to win the big ones. This is not hypocrisy; it is tact. It clear the decks for a clean fight when the big issue does come up. Then, if you lose, you can do it with self-respect; and if you win you will be on the road to forcing respect from a community that wanted to withhold it. It is one thing to risk your post for a breach of local etiquette; it is quite another to risk it for what you regard as truth.

A second difficulty the teacher faces lies in his social position. This varies inversely with the prosperity of the place in which he teaches: in a really impoverished village he is likely to be on top of the heap, while in a wealthy suburb he may be regarded as a superior nursemaid. In the average American town, however, his position tends to be anomalous. His superior education and traditional gentility may prevent his association on equal terms with those in whose proximate income class he falls. On the other hand, his comparatively low income may prevent his association with men and women of analogous education who have become successful business men or taken up one of the better paid professions. The result is that he tends to associate too much with his own kind. He eats his lunches at the school cafeteria with his fellows; he invites, and is invited by, them to dinner parties; he even takes his vacations with them. There is nothing wrong with the society of teachers; the difficulty arises when it is made an exclusive diet. Plumbers associate with butchers and lawyers with physicians, but teachers largely only with each other. The result is an over-preponderance of shop-talk with its emphasis on detail. One way to lessen this danger is occasionally to risk your lunch money away from the school cafeteria. Another way to lessen it is to face squarely the fact that your income is smaller than that of other similarly educated groups and that everyone knows it is. No man you might really want to associate with would let this difference in income stand in both your ways unless a false pride prompted you to embarrass him with hospitalities he knows you cannot afford.

The ultimate way to avoid the danger of becoming narrow is to leave teaching. I do not mean this as a counsel of despair or as a joke. In order to develop a broad, well-informed teacher, I can think of no better prescription than to leave the profession for a year or two early in your career and to earn your living in some totally different way —as a secretary, a store clerk, a farmhand. This is valid advice especially for those who have gone directly into teaching after four years of college and with virtually no experience of life outside of academic places. It is almost the only valid way to achieve a realistic perspective on your job and its social significance. It may also show you—by contrast—how extraordinarily pleasant the life of a teacher can be.

But not only can the life of a teacher be pleasant; it can present opportunities for development of the individual that no other profession has. Any professional may become so wrapped up in his work that he sees the world only from his own corner. The teacher has least excuse for such narrowness, for he has more time away from his job than any other professional has.

Most schools are closed twenty of the year's fifty-two weeks. The vacations should be used to face outward from the job, to experience something new. And by "something new," I do not mean listening to a series of lectures or visiting five countries in a six-weeks' tour of Europe. Although study and travel are two obvious ways for a teacher to spend a summer vacation, if he can afford them, they must be more than an extended travelog or a series of lyceum lectures. Here are some do's and don't's about summer travel:

1. Don't go on a conducted tour unless it is for some specific purpose like a study of housing conditions or of the drama and is led by a reputable authority in that field.

2. Travel alone or with only one or two companions. Larger groups often do more things for less money, but you spend too much time with your kind and it is all too safe and comfortable to be much more than a prolonged picnic.

3. Don't visit more than one or two countries and don't move about constantly within those two. Railroad stations, tourist hotels, and monuments are the accidents of a civilization. A month as a house-holder in a Dorset village will give you a better understanding of English life and psychology than two months of buses and bargains.

4. Visit no large countries whose language and civilization you have not studied. Know just why you are going

and what you expect to find. Your experience will still be unexpected enough.

And here are some do's and don't's about summer study —particularly at university summer sessions:

1. Think of the summer as an opportunity to travel and live in different surroundings almost as much as it is strictly an academic experience. Choose your institution not merely for the courses it has to offer, but also because it is in New York or Berkeley or Grenoble. Then register for a course light enough to let you explore ways of living in new surroundings.

2. Summer sessions are usually too short and the classes too large to train experts. Their academic function is introduction to new ideas and review. In England they are called "refresher courses." Therefore you should plan to do your really serious advanced study either by yourself or during a year's leave of absence if you can afford it.

3. Do not confine your courses to lectures on education. Not only should you broaden your interests, but you should avoid, for reasons mentioned earlier in this chapter, a companionship made up exclusively of teachers.

Both study and travel take money, and you may not be able to save enough out of the small salary most beginners receive. You may, particularly the first few years, find it absolutely necessary to support yourself by earning money during the summer. Many young teachers meet such an emergency by securing a position in a summer camp—a good idea if you do not do it too often. The routine, the confinement, and the relationship with children at a summer camp is not so different from that at school as to develop new facets of your personality. Others, failing to qualify for camp posts, earn a less agreeable living in a shop, office, farm, or factory. Such jobs, while they may not be so healthy as camp, can still turn out to be disguised blessings.

The modern teacher, the one who is alert, courageous,

and capable of understanding the life around him with other than academic insight—in other words, the teacher who will never be called schoolmarm—must have first-hand experience of the non-academic life.

I have suggested above that it is wise to leave the profession at least for one year during your early career. If circumstances make this impossible, then the least you can do is to step into other shoes for a summer. I have tried office, farm, and factory myself and know that the fresh types of contact, the new understanding of "routine," the totally different ways of looking at life such experiences afford, are each worth several summer sessions of lectures.

Whatever activities you engage in outside of school work, whether during summer holidays or not, play their part in keeping the hallmark of the profession off you and therefore in making you a better teacher. Whether it is political work, string quartets, or even selling magazine subscriptions, there is the chance to develop those sides of you which are not professionally "teacher." All such activities are obviously not equally valuable. Gardening probably is a better hobby to have than bridge. What is most necessary, however, is to have *some* outside interests. For teaching, while it can be the best way in the world to earn a living, can also be social, intellectual, and emotional stagnation.

Chapter 6

Your Future

As to pay, Sir, I beg leave to assure the Congress that as no pecuniary consideration could have tempted me to accept this arduous employment at the expense of my domestic ease and happiness, I do not wish to make any profit from it.
— WASHINGTON, on his appointment as Commander-in-chief
— But there's a gude time coming.
— SCOTT

IN A BURST OF CONFIDENCE, the mother of a high school graduate once told me that she was sending her daughter to a normal school because "teaching for a year or two before marriage is such a *respectable* thing to do."

That is the way too many teaching careers are born—or rather, stillborn. This particular girl got a husband long before she got a job; but thousands of young women enter what is optimistically called the teaching "profession" each year with one, if not both, eyes on the main chance—a young man able and willing to support them. If they succeed in landing their fish within four or five years, they have served an inattentive apprenticeship; if they fail and keep on failing, they learn to rationalize their desire for a home and children and become either sour old maids or dear old things with a penchant for redirecting the sticky molasses of thwarted affection over the heads of their academic charges. That is how schoolmarms are made.

The initial trouble lies in the unprofessional attitude of the beginner. No one would think of entering law or medicine for two or three years as "a stepping stone to something better," like marriage. Men make the same mistake, though not with a career of marriage in mind. They often enter teaching because the initial salary is comparatively good and because they are "waiting for something better to turn up." They then stick—literally stick—in the job because they do not realize that even a barrel hoop will not turn up without being stepped on, and because after a while they get married and cannot afford to adventure on something else. Such young people are doing favors neither to themselves, to their pupils, nor to those teachers who are genuine professionals. They will be discouraged from teaching only when all teachers are required by law to attain a master's degree before being allowed to practise, as secondary school teachers now are required to in California and in some few other states. Then teaching will not be so commonly regarded as a respectable cold storage plant for unripe young things.

I am not arguing against marriage for teachers. On the contrary, I believe that a happily married man or woman, one who is well adjusted sexually and socially, who has faced squarely and solved with some success the problems of budget and of living with a member of the opposite sex, and who understands intimately the parent-child relationship, is more likely to make a good teacher than another. Those communities which used to refuse teaching posts to married women may have had some economic arguments on their side but showed little educational sense.

The economic arguments these communities had on their side—arguments that still affect the comparative salaries of men and women in many fields, especially in business—are that, after a very few years, a much larger percentage of women than of men give up their jobs in favor of marriage, and therefore their years of learning on the job should not be paid so well as men's. Furthermore, there is a general feeling—well justified, too—that the preponderance of women teachers in our schools, a ratio today of about four to one, is unfortunate, and in order to attract more men into the profession, they must be paid better. Today, however, the equal-pay-for-equal-work slogan has penetrated into the schools; and while it is still true that the higher-paid administrative jobs go more often to men than to women, very few, if any, salary schedules are published with a sex differentiation.

The cheerful fact is that today, more than ever before in the United States, the sad story of the grossly underpaid teacher is fading. It was certainly a vivid story as long ago as 1870, when the average annual salary for teachers, principals, and supervisors combined was an almost incredibly low $189. By 1929, this figure had risen to about $1,400—still very sad, but almost identical with the average earnings of every American working for a wage or for a salary. But things started to improve for the teaching profession after World War II, and by 1954, teachers were averaging $4,012 and others only $3,830.

How do these figures compare with the earnings of the non-teaching professionals, that is, the doctors and lawyers (but not the ministers and actors)? Not so well at first glance. Non-salaried doctors and lawyers in 1929 were averaging $5,152 a year; in 1954 this figure had risen to $11,421. But even here, notice that the percentage rise for the general non-salaried professionals was 122 per cent; for the teachers it was 187 per cent.

And there are these factors to be weighed into the comparison: (1) a very large number of the teachers did not have college degrees and pitifully few of them had had training equal in length and thoroughness to that required for an M.D.; (2) the salaries of the teachers represented pay for only about thirty-two weeks of work a year, and (3) in projecting the economic benefits of positions comparatively, one must take into consideration such matters as security and fringe benefits on which self-employed professionals almost always come off second best.

But in gross income it is still true today—and will continue to be so in the foreseeable future—that teachers average less well than the best paid of the other professions, that is, medicine and law as opposed to the ministry.

The average salary for teachers in 1962-63 was close

to $5,000; the average total of fees collected by lawyers and doctors the same year was something approaching double that. However, if one were to deduct the non-teaching professions' overhead expenses in earning these fees, the two averages would be much closer. Furthermore, such wide averaging means little in any given case. For example, the average pay for schoolteachers in the far west was over $7,000 in the same year that teachers in the southeast averaged about $4,600.

All that averaging can show is that, in general, the financial (along with the educational and the social) status of teachers has been improving over the years. An illustrative example may be more striking. Three springs ago, a young friend of mine was graduated from a Long Island college with a B.A. and started teaching French in a Long Island junior high school the following fall. Her salary was $4,500, the standard beginner's salary in that town. By chance, this was precisely the same salary that, after twenty years experience, I—along with many associate professors at "rich" Columbia University—was earning when I left teaching in 1940. If she had stayed in the public school teaching, there is no telling where she might have gone. The superintendency of schools in New York carries a salary of $35,000 a year; in Chicago it is even higher. But this story has a different ending, harking back to an earlier paragraph, where I mentioned some of the deplorably old-fashioned notions of old-fashioned schoolboards. My young friend met a nice, prosperous young businessman, and Long Island has lost a potentially fine teacher.

On the college level the story regarding salaries is a little different, but also very encouraging. Beginners are likely to be graduate students doing not nearly so well as my young friend. Even so, they are relatively much better off than the entire dramatis personae of a play written by Edna Ferber and George Kaufman in the early 1920's. The play was about the social and economic problems of college professors—full professors—and the title reflected the average wage. It was called *$1,200 A Year.*

In 1960 (the latest figures I have) the median salary of college teachers of all grades, from instructors to full professors, was $6,711 and of full professors alone, $9,107. This may not seem very high when one considers the amount of training and experience required to become a full professor. But the most striking development in the past few years has been the salaries commanded by the very top of the profession, that is, by men who, as scientists, lawyers, or administrators could be earning large sums off a college campus. More and more professors have a base salary today upwards of $20,000 in the larger universities, while university presidents may do even better than superintendents of large school systems.

The picture, in short, is much rosier than it has ever been. Yet it is true that a really ambitious young college graduate can be earning more, albeit with less security, ten years after college if he does not become a teacher. This combination of security with comparatively low rewards helps make schoolmarms of teachers.

In a vague way, the general public realizes this fact. Most men who have taught ten years or more have heard the successful alumnus who is earning twice as much as they are, ask with an ill-concealed patronage, "Oh, are you still teaching?" As much as to say, "You used to give promise of something better than *that.*" The American attitude towards the male teacher has always been at best tinged with contempt partly because he has, in "a land of opportunity," limited his own financial opportunities, and partly because he is regarded as competing chiefly with women.

When our tradition of rugged individualism becomes only a memory, when the secure if unaffluent income of the teacher becomes comparatively attractive, and when a larger number of capable men are attracted to the profession, male teachers may obtain from a dying Babbittry the respect they have long enjoyed on the European continent, but not much before. If you value that respect, it is well to note that it grows in proportion to the age of your pupils. The middle school has more prestige than the elementary; the secondary school more than the middle; and the average college professor earns approximately the same respect as a rather unsuccessful physician. Should you achieve the status of, say, the director of a government-sponsored scientific project in a university, yours may well surpass the respect accorded, say, a state senator but probably not that of a U.S. senator. While, if you are called from your university to become a cabinet member or even to inhabit the general purlieus of the White House or the Pentagon, you may achieve the slings and arrows of outrageous public life. But by that time you will be less a professional teacher and more nearly a professional politician. Generally speaking, however, you can pretty accurately measure the respect you receive from a business civilization in dollars and cents. The true professional lets this fact bother him about as much as it bothers the true artist.

From the economic point of view, the older the children you teach, the better off you are likely to be. The senior high school teacher averages about $500 a year more than the elementary school teacher. On the other hand, it is generally easier to become an administrator in the elementary school—particularly if you have a graduate degree —than in the high school, and administrators are paid more than classroom teachers. As for college teaching, the initial rewards are likely to be smaller than in high school, but there is a better chance of a good salary later on. It is also much easier to go from college teaching to high school or from high school to elementary than vice versa.

These are the hard facts which many educational writers would like to alter. They point out that according to modern psychology the kindergarten and primary teacher really does a far more responsible and delicate job than the high school teacher and, accordingly, ought to be paid at least as much. Their premise is doubtless right, but their conclusion is at this stage of the game economically unsound. As things are now, it still takes a higher degree of scholarship and hence more preparation to get a job teaching an academic subject on the high school or college level than to secure the professional training of an elementary school teacher. And if we paid people according to the importance of their jobs, sewer cleaners would get much more than stock-brokers. Perhaps that would be a good thing.

Don't blink the hard facts; neither let them overwhelm you. Generally speaking, it is probably better at the beginning to aim at as high an academic level as possible, simply because, as I have said, it is easier to go down than up. It is also probably wise, during your first ten years, to get experience of teaching at various age levels. But more important than any of these considerations is finding the place for which you are best fitted. I have seen excellent primary school teachers force their way into high school and be miserable failures; I have seen first-rate classroom teachers become second-rate administrators. Such occurrences are expensive little tragedies paid for by the teacher's sense of failure and by mishandled children.

It is the teacher's job to be an expert in whatever subject he teaches and to earn the respect of others despite a comparatively low salary. A part of this respect is earned by his expertness; more is earned by his being the sort of person a community is forced to respect; but it is still necessary for him to act cooperatively with other teachers to raise the status of the profession. This is not done by playing bridge and eating dinners with them. It is done by working in professional organizations, by helping to define professional standards, by contributing to the scholarship of education, and, when necessary, by acting politically with his fellows for the advancement of the profession as a whole. Until he develops a pride in, and respect for, his own work, he will never earn the respect of others.

Interlude on Parents

The parent who could see his boy as he really is, would shake his head and say, "Willie is no good: I'll sell him."
—STEPHEN LEACOCK

THIS THEN, is what I think it means to be a teacher.

Before going into the classroom to discuss how to be one, I should like to say a word about problems sometimes created by parents. Most parents present no direct problem at all: they stay comfortably far from the school for the greater part of the year, and when they do come into contact with teachers are gentle and helpful. Unfortunately it is the exception who will stand out in your experience—the parent who is stupid, selfish, or downright mean. He will probably not come your way more often than once a year, but when he does he must be dealt with firmly.

A young friend of mine during her first year of teaching was persecuted by a boy who had a crush on her. This crush did not take the usual comparatively harmless form of perpetual offers of service in and out of school, sentimental letters, and preposterous excuses for "conferences." Instead, he used to call her on the telephone at night and without giving his name pose as an ardent but unknown admirer. For a long time Miss F. did not know who the nuisance was; but as he did not appear to be sufficiently discouraged by repeated snubs, she had to get the assistance of a telephone company official to trace the calls.

At first she could not decide whether to be annoyed or amused; but when the boy denied all knowledge of the calls in the face of the letter from the telephone company, she asked his father to come to school to see her. She might, of course, have asked the principal of the school to deal with the situation, but that, she thought, would be weak of her. When the father came and was told of his son's antics on the telephone, he smiled in a tolerant way. "I knew it all the time," he said. "You know what boys are like, Miss F." (She was rapidly learning, she thought— and parents too.) "You can hardly blame Jim. In fact, I could go for you in a big way myself."

"Then," says Miss F. in telling the story, "I did call in the principal."

A fantastic story, you will say, and so it is. But it happens to be true, and you will find few experienced teachers who cannot match it. The simple fact is that few parents— even those who themselves have been teachers—know what schooling is all about; and still fewer—even those who want to most—can see problems from the teacher's point of view and give help rather than hindrance. If you will assume ahead of time that parents will *mis*understand, you can be only pleasantly disappointed.

It is in the nature of things that this should be so. If you will remember that the school is an agent of the State, that its function is to train boys and girls to become grown-up citizens, you will see why. The family (and here it is most frequently represented by the mother) regards its children as members of the family, primarily if not exclusively. But as the child grows up, it becomes more and more a citizen of the state; the school regards it as an individual who can or should learn to stand on his own feet; and the better the child succeeds, the weaker grows the family's hold. It has served its function. Naturally it gives up its hold with extreme reluctance; for once it has lost its hold, the family begins to break up.

Now all this sounds as though the parent were the natural enemy of the teacher—and so he is, up to a certain point. Plato recognized this fact over two thousand years ago and proposed a radical solution: he wanted to have the state take children away from their parents so early that they would not know each other when the children grew up. But even the U.S.S.R. has not found it necessary to be as radical as Plato.

The fact is that few parents understand this natural pull in opposite directions, for it becomes obvious on comparatively rare occasions. On the contrary, almost all parents are anxious to have Johnny do well at school and profess a sincere eagerness to do everything to help the teacher. They will help with Johnny's homework (sometimes even too much), they will make costumes for the school play, they will supervise social gatherings, they will consult with the teacher, they will even invite him to dinner.

And what should you do about these proffers of help? First of all remember the possible dangers they present— the dangers that the parents may, with the best intentions in the world, be offering indirect bribes for the preferential treatment of their own children and towards securing an undue influence on the general educational policy of the school. These dangers are by no means always real, but they are potentially there and must be guarded against by circumspection.

Remember, too, the natural pull that there is between parents and the school; and when you come across a parent who wishes to keep her child on leading strings too long, do not blow up but summon all the tact and understanding you have been blessed with by birth and experience. After all, parents have a large stake in the process of education, their role is an extremely difficult one, and their offers of help are usually genuine and, often as not, disinterested. Therefore accept them whenever you can with a clear conscience.

Accept them and try to get more. Try to work in with the parent-teacher association, or to form one if the school does not already have it. And do not make that association a series of formal meetings for the discussion of abstract educational problems or for airing the peculiarities and difficulties of individual boys and girls. That would be to run the triple risk of having the association dissipate itself with boredom, blow up in personalities, or—worst of all—take the school management out of the hands of the teachers. Rather, invite the parents to have a good time with you, in the shop, in the gymnasium, on picnics. Invite them to see school exhibits and school plays. Then get into your pupils' homes and do and discuss all sorts of things with their parents. Some of them will be bores, of course; but others will be the means of your looking outward from your profession, of making contacts in professional, artistic, business, and political circles that should enrich you as a person and make you a better teacher. As a teacher, you almost always will be spending your time profitably on such occasions, for these reasons:

First of all, you will get to know your pupils better—and in a way you cannot possibly get to know them in the classroom. To see the conditions under which they have to work, to understand the basic social assumptions of their family background, to get an inkling of the emotional tie-ups which exist between parents and children, between brother and sister, is to handle your own charges just that much more intelligently. It also enables you to make your teaching just that much more alive. Is Father in the tobacco business? Use that fact in Johnny's geography assignments. Is big brother airplane-crazy? Get him to explain some of the scientific principles involved. Does the family have a favorite television show watched week after week? Use it as an exercise in critical composition.

But even more important, you will be able to get the family to work with you instead of against you. Your visit to the family, your contacts at school will always be something of an occasion; and if you can insinuate, suggest, or even assert what might be done for Johnny, you can at least be fairly sure of an attentive audience—*and* a powerful one. For in a day school at least, the influence of the family usually is far stronger than the influence of the school, however much we teachers would like to flatter ourselves that it is the other way around. The children are with you, say, six hours out of the twenty-four, and then only about half the days of the year. So, in so far as possible, get the family working with you, as it usually is only too anxious to. It is an enormous force for good or evil, and little of the time spent with it is wasted.

Never, never let it get to the point where Mama says, "I think *I* know what is best for *my* child." The chances are she doesn't, for a parent *ipso facto* is an amateur and a teacher *ipso facto* is a professional. But it doesn't do to point out this distinction, or to insist that she would not dream of saying any such thing to her physician. It would be too easy for her to retort that she *asks* her physician's advice when she *needs* it, and then what could you say? No, if you have let it get to this point, you have probably made some tactical blunder, and your best plan is to step gracefully aside and let the matter rest for about a year. When you meet next, you may both be feeling better.

Parents, then, are your most powerful potential enemies and your most powerful potential allies—almost always more powerful than you are yourself. My advice is to size up each case quite cold-bloodedly, quite professionally, and then turn it to the best possible advantage for yourself and for your pupils.

PART II

Chapter 7

Preparing Lessons and Facing the First Class

Oh, Sairey, Sairey, little do we know what lays before us!
— DICKENS

FACING YOUR VERY FIRST CLASS is like going on your very first "date," or like making a stage debut. It may be preceded by sleeplessness, inability to eat, and breaking out in sweat; and when you actually face the class your tongue may stick so tenaciously to the roof of the mouth that you think you will need a chisel and hammer to loosen it.

Somehow or other it comes loose, the sweat subsides, and before the period is over you have the feeling that everything is going beautifully—you can't wait till you meet the class again. I have known this to happen even to young teachers who gave appallingly bad first performances, who would have done much better if only their tongues *had* stuck to the roofs of their mouths. There is some dramatic attraction in that first experience, in seeing carefully prepared teaching material actually take shape in a classroom, which gives most of us an emotional lift however modestly we may appraise our own performance objectively.

Whether it is the first class of a career or just the first meeting of an experienced teacher with a new class, there is bound to be a certain amount of nervousness on the part of a conscientious man or woman. In small amounts, it is a healthy emotion: it indicates that the teacher has not become too blasé to improve. Yet it is not an agreeable emotion in the beginning, and there are several things you can do to lessen it, though never, I hope, to eliminate it completely.

First of all, do not seek and take too much advice from experienced teachers. It will only make you more nervous, as does too much advice when you are about to hit a golf ball. I remember my own first encounter with a practice class. (The word "encounter" is used advisedly.) My supervisor, as I was about to enter the door, said, "Now remember: you either win or lose your class through their first impression of you." I lost it. It was a group of ninth-grade boys in a New York slum district, and my assigned task was to introduce them to the delights of the *Odyssey* in translation. Still, I am sure that the failure of my class was the fault as much of my supervisor as of Homer or myself. Her advice was sound enough so far as it went; but it came at precisely the wrong moment. It should have come much earlier or not at all.

A class does size you up on your first meeting and is likely to stick by its first impression even though the newness of the situation may have given it a false one. Therefore it is a good idea to turn the tables and give the class something to do almost at once. If they are writing or reciting and you are guiding and correcting, they will have less opportunity for passing judgments and you more. That is as it should be. Furthermore, it will give the class the immediate impression that you mean business—a very good idea for them to have.

Too many young teachers take over the lecture method they clearly remember from college and outline in the first class what they hope to do the rest of the term. Elaborate introductions are boring for young pupils, and seldom remembered. It is almost indispensable to good teaching for a class to know just what is expected of it and what they may plan to accomplish, but if you can seem to draw the information out of them and let them help develop the plans, you will secure much more cooperation than if you give a predigested outline.

A detailed, predigested outline is likely to be bad in any case, unless you have a good previous knowledge of the class. Careful planning is essential to good teaching, but you cannot plan intelligently without knowing not only what you are going to teach but the human beings to whom you are going to teach it. If you can observe the class at least once before you meet it yourself, if you can get to know a few of its members at least slightly, if you only know some of their names, the first meetings will be easier and more effective. The material for a first class is pretty nearly certain to be carefully prepared: nervousness guarantees that; but it may be prepared in such detail that it is not easily readapted to the needs of your particular class as they reveal themselves.

There is a well known story ascribed I believe, to Barett Wendell, of Harvard. When he gave his first lecture, he had it carefully outlined on cards and nicely calculated to last exactly an hour. As he lectured, he put the top card at the bottom of the pile and so worked slowly through the pack. Presently he found himself faced again with the first card, and, glancing at the clock, found that only twenty minutes had passed. Nervousness had made him talk more quickly in the lecture room than in the rehearsals. There was only one thing he could think of doing —start all over again. He did this and went through the cards three times without the class's knowing the difference.

This is an example of preparing material carefully without actually preparing a class. Every teacher early in his career must have some experience of the sort, and if it happens frequently it becomes a nightmare: what shall I do if I run out of material? There are several lessons to be learned from it:

First, one has never prepared a class adequately if one has organized only the teaching material and has not visualized pretty completely just what is going to happen in the classroom—what the pupils as well as the teacher are likely to do, say, and feel.

Second, it is wise always to have much more material available than one plans to use. Then, if things go differently from the way they have been visualized—as they often do and should—it is comparatively easy to change. The unused material can always be used another day or with another class.

Third, a class can be prepared for too elaborately. If that happens—particularly if one does not know the class well—any departure from the schedule that an unexpected question or other interruption occasions may upset plans so badly that the hour is a failure.

A beginner does well to prepare in some detail, though with provision for changing plans at the last minute or during the course of the lesson. Backed with careful notes, he feels much more confidence. As he gets more experience and comes to know the class better, he should prepare fewer and fewer notes. They become unnecessary and only stand in the way of fluidity. This does not mean that the experienced teacher should try to get along without preparation. It means rather that he will prepare in larger units than a single class. He will organize materials for, say, a six-week outline of work and alter his plans from day to day to fit the current needs of his particular group.

Yet there is danger here too. In thinking of his work in larger units, the teacher may easily forget that each period ought to be an artistic whole. I have seen experienced history and geography teachers, relying on a prescribed text, divide the work for a term into ten-page assignments and stick to those evenly divided doses regardless of how they chopped up the chapters or of how well the previous ten pages had been mastered. This may be hard to believe, but it is all too common a practice. Any plan for teaching, whether it is for a whole term or just for half an hour, should be an artistic job: it should have a beginning, a middle, and an end; it should have its points of high interest well spaced, and it should leave as few untied ends as possible. This artistic shape cannot be planned for in every detail, as a rigid scheme for either a long or a short period is almost certain to be a partial misfit for the human beings who constitute the class, however well it may fit the subject matter. I like to think of the art of teaching as being somewhat analogous to the art of the old improvisors on the piano who, given certain thematic material, would improvise for a given time, fitting their composition to the mood and circumstances, giving it shape as they went along, but leaving the details to the dictates of an inspiration grounded in a sensitive feeling for their medium.

The greatest pleasure in our art comes, I think, from knowing what it is you want to do, having a large fund of material from which to draw, and adapting it to a particular class as you get to know it—exploring here, giving additional emphasis there, bringing in new highlights, making fresh applications, and coming gradually to sense the reciprocal relationships between the academic and the human material with which you are working.

It is surprising how many young teachers appreciate these possibilities almost at once and derive keen pleasure from making the most of them. There are a hundred details and aspects to the art, and I should like to devote a rather long chapter to discussing a few of them.

Chapter 8

How to Make a Class Interesting, or The Art of Teaching

Uniting, by an honest art,
The faithful monitor's and poet's part,
Seek for delight that they may mend mankind,
And, while they captivate, inform the mind.
—COWPER

A FUNDAMENTAL DIFFERENCE between an art and a science is that the former assumes an audience and requires a style—a style to interest the audience. That is why physics is a science but the teaching of physics is an art. The art most like teaching is drama, with the teacher in the role of both playwright and actor. There is this important difference, however: the audience in a theatre is passive, and Tuesday night's show is almost identical with Wednesday's. In a classroom, the pupils take a part in the production that is as great as or greater than the teacher's. He may set the stage and preconceive the general outline of the play, but the class will have much of the important dialogue and action, and one can never be sure how the story is going to come out.

Another important difference is that a play closes when it ceases to interest audiences. The school goes on and on to the end of term, and the poor pupils do not even have the option of walking out during the performance if they are bored. Compulsory attendance makes teachers forget their moral obligation to be interesting. Pity and respect for one's pupils ought to make one remember; so ought respect for the art of teaching. But what should be the strongest incentive is the fact that a pupil cannot learn well if he is not interested. If a school bores its pupils, its only function can be that attributed to it by Shaw—to keep children out of the way of their elders for a few hours a day.

It is not enough to quote Buffon's "The style is the man himself" and assume that if you are an interesting person you will make an interesting teacher, if not you won't. Like most aphorisms, Buffon's is only a half-truth when taken out of its original context. Style requires technique and practice. You cannot be a successful playwright or actor simply by having the foresight to be born an interesting person. You must master these arts and their styles, and so it is with teaching.

Let us see what the raw materials of the art of teaching are and how an interesting style may be developed.

The elements involved are your own personality, that of your pupils, the subject matter or skills you teach, and the interaction of these elements, which is the lesson itself. Some forethought given to each of these may help enormously.

Certain aspects of our personality—like height and good looks—we cannot do much about, and yet they must be taken into consideration in forming a style. If you have the sort of animal magnetism or charm that attracts boys and girls, you can afford to occupy a much more prominent place on the stage than if you have not. It is foolish to pass over this question with mock modesty. Every intelligent person has some fairly accurate idea of his own physical attractiveness; and if he is not sure how he impresses a group of children, a few sessions in a classroom will tell him. If he is naturally retiring and ineffective in the centre of the stage, he will have to develop a more subtle technique: the class will play the more obviously prominent part and he will control it from the background. Every good teacher should have a bit of the actor in him and use particularly that portion of it which is called audience sense. The too obviously attractive person always runs the danger of charming himself more than his class; the retiring person may exaggerate what he considers his deficiencies and encounter each class with the negative prayer that they may behave rather than the positive one that he may interest.

Another personal qualification over which we do not have much control is speed of mind. The exceptionally fast-witted teacher runs the danger of being always so far ahead of his class that he loses patience waiting for it to catch up. Yet the man who says that he could never be a teacher because he has not the patience, does not understand the problem. However brilliant his wits, they must not be employed exclusively on the subject matter with which he presumably is already quite familiar, but rather on seeing whether his pupils have mastered it and on making it interesting enough for them to do so if they have not. Brains are no disqualification for teaching. If, however, yours is the type of mind that moves slowly and is not able to cope with virtually any unexpected development, the implication for you is extremely careful planning for each lesson. This is especially so in your first two or three years of teaching any given subject matter. After a sufficient time you will have found a way of dealing with practically anything: "unexpected situations" have a way of repeating themselves.

Speech is the most important of the personal elements over which we have some control. A bad—even an excellent—voice can always be made better. So can enunciation. The more scholarly type of young teacher is likely to overlook his own vocal shortcomings, thinking that what he has to say is far more important than the instrument which says it. He is too much the playwright, too little the actor, and forgets that Shakesepare's most musical speeches can easily become tedious on the stage. Actors rehearse regularly; there is no reason why a teacher should not do so occasionally. It would not be a bad idea for you some time to drop in at one of the shops that make individual phonograph records and listen to yourself present your favorite theorem in Euclid or even give instructions for observing the fire drill regulations. Try it without rehearsing.

Such a record should also teach you something about your own pitch and rhythm of speech. A regular growl is bad, a whine is bad, a squeak is bad, a sing-song is bad, a telegraph-code staccato is bad—in fact any regular, easily predictable pattern is bad. Rhythm and pitch should be suggested by the content: when you are formulating a rule in arithmetic, you should not sound exactly the same way as when you are reading out examples. Yet most teachers acquire a regular classroom formula for speech that scarcely varies from one year's end to the next. Improvement does not necessarily require the services of a speech expert. An impartial observer such as a principal, supervisor, or fellow teacher can usually point out defects that you are not aware of. It may even be possible (though individuals vary widely in this regard) for you to be able to help yourself by listening to your own voice.

There is not much use in advising you about diction. The careful mind will choose words well, the careless one will not, and that is pretty nearly all there is to it. You can help yourself considerably, however, by preparing verbatim before any given class a few of the sentences you will use. To prepare more than a few is likely to lead you into lecturing, usually a dull business anywhere below college level. At the very least, get yourself off to a good start by knowing what you are going to say when you enter the room, even if it is only a routine request.

For instance, it is much better to begin, "We will start at page fifty-nine" than, "Let me see, where are we? Oh yes. We got through those last two pages and that brings us to somewhere about fifty-nine. That's right, isn't it? Yes, fifty-nine."

Dress is another detail of personality that the more scholarly type of teacher too often disregards. If he stopped long enough to realize the intimate way in which one's clothes—one's hair and fingernails too—proclaim one's self-respect, he might give it more attention. The traditional figure of the long-haired, absent-minded, and grease-spotted scholar was a self-debasing figure who said to his classes in effect: "I am of no importance whatsoever. All that counts is my Greek roots. Disregard me, step on me— it really makes very little difference." It may make very little difference in a graduate seminar, but not in a school-room. Pupils acquire interest almost always through the teacher, and they cannot do it through a teacher who commands no respect because he does not respect himself. I am, of course, not advocating extremes in style, but a level of scrupulous decency approximately that of your pupils' parents or better. Interest in your appearance should never be allowed to interfere with interest in the lesson as it can with either the sloppy scholar or the fashion plate.

The most important personal element in making a class interesting is your own enthusiasm for your subject. For young pupils at least, interest is very much a matter of contagion, and it will be hard for them to catch it from you if you do not have it or if you hide it under a supercilious show of boredom. Nothing is more deadening than the attitude of the young teacher who, finding himself having to teach the elementary aspects of a subject in which he has been doing advanced work, says to his class with what he considers healthy frankness: "Now this is really completely boring; but you'll have to go through with it because it is in the syllabus, and maybe some day if you stick at it long enough you will find out why." Others act less explicitly but equally disastrously by letting such an attitude be sensed by the class.

If, however, you honestly feel that way about the more elementary aspects of your subject, there are two things you can do:

First, you can drum up an artificial enthusiasm in yourself. This, for a short time, is not so hard to do as you may think. Find some detail that does have interest, however superficial, and play it up. It is a device that in the long run will not work and would be a form of downright dishonestly if it did. It may serve, however, for one or two difficult situations and tide over a time when you feel you are losing your class.

Second, stop to analyse your subject not from the point of view of what interests you but from the point of view of what interests boys and girls. This is much more genuine. You will find it difficult to interest high school pupils in differing theories as to how Chaucer's lines were read in the fourteenth century; you will find it easier to interest them in what Chaucer ate and how, in the sports of his time and the ways of fighting.

Memorizing French conjugations is probably fun for no one, but it can be made considerably more interesting by showing what happens to some of the forms in modern French slang. This is not a plea for cheap popularization. It is only a reminder that children are likely to be more interested in living than in books, and that the way to get them to understand the vitality of books is to demonstrate their relationship to living. No reasonably intelligent person likes every detail of his job, and one always tends to discount unqualified enthusiasm for a many-faceted thing like a subject of study. Any large work, whether it is the mastery of a musical instrument, the making of a sociological survey, or the building of a bridge, involves a certain amount of drudgery which, taken by itself, is not much fun.

Difficulty in interesting a class usually comes from the fact that the pupils see only the drudgery; an understanding of learning's purpose is confined to the teacher—and he may see it only from his own point of view.

This brings us to the second of the elements involved in making your teaching interesting—the subject matter. One of the few almost universally agreed upon tenets of modern educational theory is that childhood is a legitimate form of existence in itself and not merely a preparation for what is optimistically called "adult life." Accordingly, there is no subject matter, with the possible exception of a few skills, that can be allowed a place in the curriculum unless it is closely bound up with the life of children. There is not much sense in giving twelve-year-olds arithmetic problems about income from stocks and bonds or in telling a high school class about the novels of Richardson because some day—in college, perhaps—they may have to read them. Children should, of course, know elementary arithmetic and how to read novels intelligently; but the arithmetic and the reading should be the sort that they *as children* have a real use for. Otherwise they become justifiably bored. The only group of teachers that seems to have a consistent respect for this principle is the shop teachers. School shops produce boats and pencil boxes, never filing cases, unless they are to be used by a school organization.

On account of college entrance requirements, tradition, or some other circumstance equally blind to the purposes of education, you may find yourself having to teach aspects of a subject that patently violate this principle. A syllabus and textbook are thrust into your hands and you are told to go to it. Probably no subject in any curriculum is so completely hopeless as all this, but take the case just the same and see what you can do.

Your course then is to take the subject matter—syllabus, textbook, and all—and enliven it with examples, analogies, parallels, even anecdotes related as closely as possible to the lives of the pupils you have in that class. Study that particular subject matter and study those particular pupils so thoroughly that you can somehow bring the two together in an interesting relationship in your daily class work. A theoretical justification of the course, to be given visiting parents, is not enough. The pupils themselves must sense that your interest in both the subject and themselves, as individuals, is genuine. Then they will associate interest and subject naturally, as you do with your constant bringing of the class work into their lives.

To do all this requires an intimate knowledge of your pupils. Theories of child psychology and the laws of learning are good to know, but they will not be of much use without knowing the lives of the particular boys and girls on your class roll. You can get one idea—and an important one—of what they are like in the classroom itself. That is not nearly enough. Almost any novel about school children, almost any child's diary, will show how little is revealed to the teacher during lesson hours. To get a more intimate understanding of school children, one should occasionally eat, talk, play, travel with them. A pupil may be a dull clod in class and possess a vivid personality on a playing field or dance floor. Seeing your charges in the fresh background of a week end in the country, a trip to Washington, or even at a class party may make them suddenly acquire a whole new perspective.

But you must not only know what their interests are; you must also know something about those interests. A whole class, or a large portion of it, may acquire a passion for stamp collecting or amateur photography. Such fads sweep over groups of children like a beneficent disease. You can almost count on a more or less universal interest in the motion pictures. If you can show your class a vivid and informed interest in their own extracurricular enthusiasms, your shared experiences will throw open a whole vocabulary of words and concepts to enliven instruction and you yourself become a fresh interest to them.

Teachers seem to many children like creatures apart, an idea that ought to be unsound. Many of us, however, justify it by assuming an air of superiority to all those unacademic concerns that really matter to children. I cannot understand what worthy dignity a teacher loses by admitting that he likes to dance or admires the acting of Laurence Oliver. But it is perfectly obvious why children consider a man dull whose only apparent interest in life is factoring or construing.

This impression of being interesting should be given

from the start, for once you achieve the reputation of being a bore (or of being unfair or sarcastic or anything else that is disagreeable) it is hard to live it down. The word gets passed round quickly, particularly about a new teacher, and what is repeated often enough is counted as fact. Fortunately, the reverse is almost equally true. If you are regarded as an interesting teacher after your first two or three classes, or if you come reputed as something of an authority in your field, an important initial skirmish is won. With a cloakroom verdict of "interesting" one must almost take pains to be dull in order to convince a class it is wrong. That is why it is a good idea to put your best foot forward first. You cannot hope to walk on that foot all year long, but it is more likely to take a step in the right direction.

These, then, are the raw materials of the art of teaching—your personality, your subject matter, your pupils. Their interaction will determine your success in achieving an interesting style, and that in turn is dependent on the same elements that make up any other art—unity, form, and rhythm.

Unity in a lesson is that quality which leaves a single definite impression with the pupils. To achieve it, one must know exactly what one wants to accomplish in that lesson and keep aiming steadily at it. The more definite the aim, the better. To engage to teach a class to "appreciate," say, Keats's "Ode to Autumn" is pretty vague; to plan to make the images of that poem as vivid as possible is far more definite. If you know that that is your object, you will not confuse it with such a one as "knowing the meaning of every word" or "being able to scan every line"—worthy enough objects, perhaps, but you cannot teach everything at the same time without destroying the unity of your lesson and with it both interest and effectiveness.

In order to achieve unity it is also necessary to keep the same underlying mood throughout. It is extremely difficult, for example, to be hilarious with a class for ten minutes and then suddenly to drop into serious discussion and expect the pupils to follow your lead. Within limits, of course, there can be variation, but there must be an underlying consistency in the atmosphere created, an atmosphere that is suggested by whatever object you have set out to accomplish. Inexperienced teachers are prone to great and pointless variation within a short space of time; old and tired ones are sometimes consistent to the point of boredom. It is variation within an underlying pattern that can make a lesson interesting and a work of art.

Given the object and the mood of a lesson, form is achieved through building up gradually toward gaining the object. A lesson should be planned so that you know where you are going, get there some time toward the close of the period, have the assignment grow naturally out of the work, and leave a short time for summary. Furthermore, the pupils should know that they have started at a definite point and ended at another farther on. A sense of going somewhere, a feeling of achievement, is one of the best guarantees of interest, and certainly one to which pupils who have worked are entitled. You may notice in yourself after certain lessons that you have a distinct sense of elation—one of the greatest satisfactions in teaching— and that after others it is not there at all. This elation (it is like walking on air) almost always comes after a lesson in which you know you have worked up to your object, perhaps with unexpected success. There has been form in that lesson.

The rhythm of a lesson will, in turn, depend upon its unity and form. Rhythm is something that almost every teacher develops individually and unconsciously, dependent partly on his natural rhythm of speech, partly, perhaps, on the state of his glands. But all sorts of far less important little things are likely to interfere with smoothness, and it is worthwhile to give them some thought.

For example, return homework exercises at the end rather than at the beginning of a lesson unless they are to form the material of instruction. The process is likely to get you off to a slow start because the pupils look through corrections and possibly compare grades. It is hard then to get going again properly. Again, you may have a more or less elaborate diagram to put on the board. Do it before you call the class to order. You may have some small pictures to illustrate your subject. Don't pass them around while you are giving other instruction, but call the class up to your desk in small groups while the rest are busy at something else. It may be necessary to rearrange furniture or to open a window. Have these things attended to swiftly and quietly before you begin teaching. It is a good idea to insist on prompt attendance, and this is easy to secure if you refuse admittance to the first two or three pupils who are tardy in a term. Lack of attention to these details will upset the rhythm and harm the interest of the class almost every time.

This, then, is the theory of making a class interesting together with a few practical precepts. But if, as I have suggested, making a class interesting is an art, then the mastery of it requires technique as well as theory. That technique includes the preparation of lessons, the use of materials of all sorts, and discipline. Yet you may master the theory and the technique but still fail to have an interesting class. Any competent music writer may compose a fugue in the manner of Bach, but the result will not necessarily be great music. In any art—and teaching is just one—real success demands mastery of theory and technique as a foundation. Beyond that no advice can help you much: you rely on inspiration, the divine spark, call it anything. If it is there, you will recognize it and you will know you have done a good job. Monday I taught a class that I know was good. The students' reactions, my feeling about it, comment I heard afterwards all told me the class was successful. Tuesday I used virtually the same notes with another group and I know the result was bad. Why the first was good and the second not, I cannot analyse. The same elements were there: the same subject matter, very similar students, and myself. One day they reacted well on each other and the next not. Perhaps I failed to build up to my main point as well, perhaps there were some irrelevant interruptions to the rhythm. Whatever it was, the experience told me again that teaching is an art, an elusive one. I have practised it long enough to know that one has good days and bad.

Chapter 9

The Two Kinds of Discipline: Keeping Order

Is there no respect of place, persons, nor time in you?
—SHAKESPEARE

Uneasy lie the heads of all that rule,
His worst of all whose kingdom is a school.
—HOLMES

THE BEGINNING TEACHER, like the old-fashioned one, is likely to think of discipline as keeping a class in order. "How is his discipline?" is a question commonly heard about teachers, meaning, Does he keep the class quiet? Do the pupils respect him? It is the question most beginners ask themselves fearfully: Will I be able to run the class, or will they run me? This kind of discipline, large as it looms in the mind of the young teacher, is really only one of two closely related kinds. The second I shall discuss in the next chapter, as the matter of keeping order may appear to be more immediately pressing.

Your old-fashioned school principal will tell you that the best way to keep order is through "moral control," which may mean anything from fear to a genuine respect based on learning and character. There is no doubt that the second is better than the first, and modern teachers rightly make every effort to banish fear from the class-room: it is all too likely to interfere with learning. But it is often difficult for a young man or woman to exhibit the necessary qualities on first facing a group of irreverent children.

My own first fulltime teaching post was in a Connecticut factory town with a really tough crew of boys and girls. Some of the boys in second year high school I felt morally certain would one day land in jail; others had already been there. To make things even less auspicious, I had been engaged as a substitute toward the end of the year—an experience like hopping on a fast-moving train and taking control. It is particularly hard when you have never seen the inside of a locomotive before. There were seven teaching periods a day, and I watched the woman whose place I was taking live through the last seven. (She was giving up teaching for marriage, she explained to me, because there would probably be less fighting.) You might have thought that the students on that last day would feel a little sentimental and make matters easy for her. But no; she had lost the respect of her classes long ago, and seven times that day, once in each class, she came to the verge of tears just begging her pupils to be quiet for one minute. By 3:30 she was thoroughly miserable. So was I.

The next morning I did, quite by accident, the best thing I could possibly have done under the circumstances. My first class was a study-hall with forty-five pupils in a room meant to seat thirty. I gave them a little talk on how to behave well. They were to study, and I wanted to study. If any disturbance was made, we would only be cheating each other, and so on and so forth. Then I sat down with a book before me pretending to study but really waiting for the show to start, my heart hammering and my mouth dry.

Within five minutes, a boy in the back of the room whispered something to his neighbor. Immediately I shot up and fairly bellowed, "Who's talking?" I hadn't intended to bellow, but somehow I had lost control of my voice. No one answered. I came down from the teacher's platform and walked menacingly down the aisle (at least I flattered myself that it was menacingly) continuing to demand that the culprit declare himself. "Anyone who talked," I said in a broken voice—broken with nervousness—"after the agreement we just made" (there had been no agreement), "is just plain low." All the time I knew exactly who had been talking, and I was praying he wouldn't admit it. What could I have done if he had? I couldn't very well start sending pupils to the principal fifteen minutes after starting my career as a teacher; and corporal punishment was not allowed in the school. Besides, he was an enormous fellow about fifty pounds heavier than I. Well, he didn't confess; and wagging my head, expressive of moral sorrow, I returned to the platform. There was no more whispering that day or any other. It must have been a pretty funny spectacle, but apparently the class was just as much frightened as I.

I have never done anything quite so melodramatic or silly since, but I failed to learn the lesson of this incident. The underlying principle is that if you have any doubt whatsoever about being able to control the class, put on a bold front and take the offensive. It does no harm to be even a little unfairly severe at first. Once you have been sized up by the class as a "strict disciplinarian," it is simple enough to ease up and make things more informal and comfortable all round, and to pull in the reins again later if, as is unlikely, the occasion should arise.

But it is almost impossible to pull in reins that you have handed over to the horse. A wise old schoolmaster pointed this fact out to me some years later, and I profited by it. In the meantime, though, I had plenty of difficulties in other schools. My next position, for example, was in a private school with a large majority of intelligent and apparently well-mannered children. The classes were all very well behaved the first day, and when a little whispering occurred on the next, I thought it would just spoil the lovely atmosphere to notice it. By the end of the next week, most of my classes were badly out of hand, and I never could tell just where I had started losing control. Between the various types of whispering, foot-shuffling, and note passing there are many apparently unobtrusive ways of breaking up a class. Before the first term was over, boys were throwing chalk, and it was only with assistance from the principal that I managed to go on at all.

Watch for small signs of inattention, deal with them severely, and the large ones will never occur. It took me several years to discover this little rule, which, known earlier, might have saved me some sleepless nights. By this time I have learned to do much better. Most teachers learn more quickly than I did; some, I am sorry to say, never.

The broncho busting or drill sergeant discipline is not the best, but neither is it the worst. Today the fashion is to cry it down, but I should call it infinitely preferable to that of an eminent scholar (now dead) who taught occasional classes in a secondary school. He was a witty man and an excellent lecturer at the University, but in his secondary school classes he was always deliberately dull so that he would not, as he put it, "court trouble with excitement." Putting children to sleep is one way of keeping them in order, but they don't learn much.

Being a drill sergeant is also better than being a dishrag. One young and untrained teacher I knew was so gentle and ineffective that when the class got completely out of hand, he could do nothing but put his head on the desk and cry. The class was first stunned—and then burst out laughing. He was too weak to recover the class and left teaching permanently at the end of the year.

It is hard to remember that a high school class usually likes a drill sergeant provided he is just and knows what he is about. The army drill sergeant knows the Infantry Drill Regulations thoroughly, and so must you know your subject if you are going to adopt his manner. It works particularly well in essentially drill classes—classes in which you are teaching spelling, principal parts, shorthand. The best exponent of the method I ever knew was an old curmudgeon of a German who taught elementary Spanish, Latin, and bookkeeping in a small town high school. He was unattractive, untidy, and stupid, but he ran his classes with so much force and zest, was so undeviatingly consistent in grading and dealing out punishments, that he had the respect of all his pupils and the real affection of some.

Nor is it necessary to be noisy or to have a loud voice. Quiet, soft-spoken tenseness will do the trick quite as well, though it is trying on the nerves if you don't naturally happen to have that sort of personality. Another teacher I know, a woman of great charm and culture, has it. She teaches physics on the west coast, and both her discussion and her laboratory classes are models of quiet, earnest busyness. At the beginning of each term she starts her first class by saying in a loud, clear voice: "Now I want everyone to know that I can speak quite as loudly as any of you, but—" and here her voice suddenly comes down to a brilliant stage whisper—"I shall not do it again this term." And she doesn't. She conducts all her classes in an extremely soft voice, the pupils leaning eagerly forward to hear what she has to say. If there is a slight sound, she will stop whatever she is doing and say calmly but dramatically, "I think s-o-m-e-o-n-e has dropped a ruler."

This Lady Macbeth type of teaching may have disastrous results with slightly deaf children in the back row, and generally speaking I should say it is rather a *tour de force* of technique than a model to be followed. I cite the illustration, however, merely as an example of the general rule that a method of keeping order should grow out of the teacher's personality. Adapt your method to yourself, and never follow another's apparently successful ways uncritically.

But drill sergeant discipline, or any similar technique, is to be recommended only as a last resort. After all, it is a leftover from the days when the best pupil-teacher relationship one might expect was a sort of armed peace. Harry East summarized it pretty well for his classmate, Tom Brown: "What one has always felt about masters is, that it's like a fair trial of skill and last between us and them—like a match at football, or a battle. We're natural enemies in school, that's the fact." But that was over a hundred years ago and the relationship between pupil and teacher has considerably changed since then. Today the relationship is—or should be—that of co-workers. Neither you nor your pupils should be aware that there is any such thing as a disciplinary problem, and you won't be if you make your lessons interesting enough and keep everyone doing something.

The amount of noise or quiet in a room is no measure whatsoever of the discipline in it. Just recently I heard a girl giving a practice lesson on paragraph structure. She had some excellent material, and the class was so much on its toes that it responded in chorus to question after question. Unfortunately she had picked up the idea somewhere that this was disorder and showed "weak discipline." "No, girls," she would say each time, "I can't understand you when you do that." However, she could understand them perfectly well, I knew, because I could. This was no "weak discipline," but a class that was so much interested, so alive and eager to work, that it could scarcely be downed. The ideal situation, I should say. That "weak discipline" was a compliment to the questioning—excellent teaching until the "No, girls, no, girls" echo vitiated it.

Everyone was busy working in that class, and that is the way it should be. Skillful questioning is, of course, not the only way to achieve this result. Reading to a class, even occasional lecturing, may have the whole class working. So, of course, may a written exercise, though even that is no guarantee. When I first took a course in "Methods of Teaching" I was told that the ideal ratio of pupil-teacher activity was 60–40. That is the sheerest nonsense. A class, if properly trained, may conduct its own discussions with virtually no help from you, as I found out when I returned to school almost speechless a few days after a tonsilectomy. There the ratio was 99–1, and it was pretty nearly the best teaching I ever did. A science demonstration which lasts throughout the period may have a ratio of 0–100; and when you use a motion picture or give a test, it is likely to be 0–0. There is no ideal ratio of pupil-teacher talking; and the ideal ratio of pupil-teacher *activity* is 100–100.

How can you be sure that everyone is working? You can't always. For all you know, the rapt gaze of the girl in the front row may be prompted by a fascinating speculation about the reliability of a half-open button on your jacket; while the brief whispering in the back of the room is the result of an inspirational idea about the lesson that just couldn't be kept in. But in general there is a feel about a class that is responding wholeheartedly quite different from one that isn't. You soon get to recognize it. Meantime, I will list a few practical suggestions that may help on occasion:

1. Don't let the same two or three pupils answer all the questions. In a discussion, try to get everyone to say at least one thing.

2. In asking questions, do not go about the room in a regular order as the pupils are seated or alphabetically. If you do that, only the pupil who is about to be called on will be likely to try to find the answer.

3. For the same reason, do not name a pupil before you ask a question. Do not say, "Jack, how much is two and two?" Rather phrase it: "How much is two and two?" (Pause while everyone's hand goes up.) "Jack?"

4. If you have any reason to think you may have trou-

ble with a class, change the seating arrangement, bringing those in the back row to the front and separating any potential troublemakers.

5. Don't sit down throughout a whole lesson unless the group is small and you are quite sure of everyone's interest. You are more impressive when you stand up, and it is easier to see what is going on.

6. Don't walk around aimlessly. It makes the pupils restless and feel like doing it too.

7. Use not only your voice to teach, but your face, hands, arms, and whole body. A good teacher must have something of the actor in him.

8. Always be ready to change your plan of procedure at short notice in case things aren't going well. A change of activity will often produce a change in tone. For an emergency measure, have a written lesson or test available for really hard nuts.

9. Never make a threat that you do not fully intend to carry out—and carry out at least one during your first week.

This list of suggestions looks pretty negative and pretty ominous—especially the last. Let me therefore append one positive suggestion, one that if followed is practically certain to make disciplinary problems vanish: *Have a good time.* The class is almost certain to take its tone from you, and if you are enjoying yourself and are interested in what you are doing, the class will be too. That is the best sort of discipline there is—the second of the two kinds I mentioned at the beginning of this chapter. It will have to have another chapter to itself.

Chapter 10

The Two Kinds of Discipline: The High Discipline of Learning

> In everything that matters, the inside is much larger
> than the outside.
>
> —G. K. CHESTERTON

THE OTHER KIND of discipline is much more difficult to describe, as it is much more difficult to attain. It has not so much to do with behavior, though that is the way it usually expresses itself, as with what goes on inside the skin. It is a matter of mind and character (but you will never get two persons to agree exactly on what mind and character are).

Roughly you will see what is meant by contrasting examples: Prospero is disciplined, Caliban not; Socrates is disciplined, Alcibiades not; a great psychiatrist is disciplined, the lunatics in his ward are not. Of course, in the old-fashioned sense we were talking about in the last chapter, Caliban and the lunatics usually are very well disciplined—but *from the outside.* The discipline of Prospero, Socrates, and the psychiatrist comes from inside the skin.

But that is only the roughest idea. There are many sorts and shades of this second kind of discipline, and not all of them are equally valuable educationally. A circus horse, for example, is very well disciplined inside the skin. The difference between him and Caliban or the lunatics is that the horse does not need to be made to do his tricks by threats of punishment or the constant surveillance of guards. He responds automatically because he has been trained to do so. A soldier in the ranks is similarly trained, only on a higher level. Even a moron may have a disciplined mind. There are many examples of morons who can do some one mental trick, like reciting a logarithmic table, with astonishing speed and accuracy. These are what we might classify as examples of low discipline. The man who can play the Brahms violin concerto *faster* than anyone else provides an example of low discipline: it takes a Szigeti, whose intonation and fluency may not be what they once were but who can balance phrase with phrase and develop the beautiful line of this composition, to provide an example of high discipline. Low discipline is the kind that lets you perform stunts—useful stunts, perhaps, but still stunts. High discipline requires the use of the finest type of mind, talent, or moral character; and I think we will see that the higher kind can never be achieved without the lower.

This rough definition of two kinds of discipline is, of course, not an adequate guide to evaluating subject matters and kinds of teaching. It will first be necessary to lay once more a ghost that continues to walk in the schools despite the most valiant efforts of modern psychologists of many different opinions. This ghost, known as "faculty psychology," holds that human beings possess different faculties like memory, reason, the passions, and the like, and that these faculties may be trained directly, through discipline. Thus, Latin was considered a good subject to study because it was hard—mastery required discipline of several "faculties." The notion was held—and is still held by many teachers, particularly in England and Germany—that by studying Latin you attained a "discipline" that could be turned on at will and spurted in any direction—ruling native tribes, for example, or directing trench warfare. And the success of England in building an empire and Germany a war machine lends, for a moment, considerable plausibility to this notion. The syllogistic reasoning would seem to run something like this:

Englishmen learn Latin.
Englishmen have built a great empire.
Therefore learn Latin to build an empire.

It may be, of course, that learning Latin and building an empire require similar abilities and training, though that would be practically impossible to prove; but to attribute a causal relationship between the two phenomena is to wrench the most extraordinary compromise out of reasoning. If learning Latin teaches you logic (another mysterious power sometimes claimed for it), it should teach it better than that. Mere "discipline" is never enough to claim for a subject. If it were, you could construct a fine curriculum out of training in crossword puzzles, balancing bottles, memorizing nonsense syllables, and tightrope walking. Latin has better claims than that.

One way psychologists have exploded faculty psychology is by showing that training is transferable from one field to another only when there are what they call "identical elements" in the two. Thus, learning the grammar of one language will help in learning the grammar of another only insofar as the two grammars are alike. Neither will help you learn geometry. Another school of psychologists will allow the possibility of a little more transfer than that. They say that the basis of transfer lies in the ability to generalize: that is, an intelligent mind may form some generalizations about languages from a study of the first and be able to apply them to the second. One might even be able to pick up some generalizations about how to study from the languages and apply them to mathematics and later to life situations. But both schools repudiate the idea that you can train some abstract quality like "reasoning power" and hope to make it function in any given situation.

Thus, in evaluating a subject matter, you must try to see just what its study will lead to. To take an obvious example, if you wish to develop your pupils' habit of looking at things for their shapes and shades, drawing would be a good subject to choose; but to confine your instruction to the technique of drawing electric light bulbs or of potted geraniums (as my elementary school teacher confined hers) is far too narrow. Once I could draw potted geraniums but not nasturtiums, and I never learned to draw a face. I have no more intelligent, disciplined idea of how to analyse a face for its planes and lines than if I had never had a drawing lesson in my life. The training was far too narrow, and I learned no generalizations about perspective and color.

Similarly, I once knew the name of every capital in the United States; but I had no idea of what a capital really is and why there are such things until I had a sound course in history that taught me the discipline of reading newspapers intelligently.

Are you going to teach arithmetic? Why? Are you going to teach music? Why? Are you going to teach physical training? Why? Each of these subjects can furnish discipline; and if you make it exclusively a low discipline, one that does not keep the higher always in mind, you might as well be teaching card tricks.

As I have suggested before, the high and broad discipline will never be achieved before the low and narrow. Szigeti could never have played the Brahms concerto as he does without first mastering scales, the intonation of double-stopping, the analysis of a composition into its parts. Steinmetz could not have performed his marvels in mathematical physics without an intimate knowledge of the logarithmic tables or the ordinary processes of calculus. Robert Louis Stevenson could not have gained his style without careful training in diction and sentence rhythms.

These, you will say, are exceptional examples, and so they are. Without his genius, no amount of low and narrow discipline will ever teach you or me to write as well as Shakespeare or to develop the fortitude of character of Andrew Jackson. But on a lower level, the principle is equally obvious. Algebra is a higher form of discipline than elementary arithmetic. Can you master the first without the second? And coming down still further, can you perform long division without multiplication and subtraction?

It is the overlooking of this point that accounts for an enormous amount of foolishness in modern educational practice. "Let the child express itself," says the half-educated follower of John Dewey and proceeds to encourage it to write symphonies and epics without knowing notes or words. Even worse is this principle when mis-applied to morals and manners. Why on earth a nine-year-old child should be encouraged to monopolize the dinner table conversation before he has been disciplined in the arts of human relations and talk, is a question that faces every adult invited to dinner by the parents of precocious and "modernly" brought-up children. Self-expression! Self-expression of what?

Yet, understanding the importance of self-expression is one of the most valuable contributions of modern educa-tion. It is only its indiscriminate application that makes one angry. For if you will regard self-expression as a mode of discipline, you will see how important it is. The child who is made to sit at his classroom desk and memorize the qualities of beet-root is undergoing discipline from the outside. The child who goes into the garden and digs about the plants, learning what makes them grow, be-coming curious over their properties, asking questions, and possibly even searching for the knowledge he wants in books, is undergoing internal discipline. Multiplication is aggravation, but not when you learn it to find out how many pounds of potatoes your school garden will produce, or to balance the books of the class shop. The child who understands—still better, *feels*—why he is learning some-thing, is undergoing an internal discipline; and what he thus learns will stay with him and make him a better person, not just a better examination-passer. Every few centuries some educator like Plato or Pestalozzi discovers the principle that one learns better when one is interested than when one is not. Sensitive teachers rediscover it every day.

Still, this can also be carried too far. When the combined

ingenuity of all the world's teachers has been expended on inventing new "projects," "correlations," "integrations," and "school journeys," there will still remain a number of elementary disciplines which such old fogies as I think children should have, and which it appears to be impossible to make them become intellectually and emotionally interested in. At least, they cannot become interested in the ultimate reasons for undergoing those disciplines. Table manners is one; foreign languages is another; taking baths is a third. Few adults and far fewer children can keep the real ultimate goal—the higher discipline—in mind long enough to make them willingly undergo the hard grind of the lower. You can have a more profitable and enjoyable time in Italy if you learn Italian first, but how many people spend two years learning the language before the trip? If you got up an hour earlier every morning to practise the piano, you could play pretty well at the end of a few years. How many do it? And if you, the adult, don't, how much more excuse is there for the child!

It is only the most exceptional person, the genius, who has such a clear, longview plan, who submits eagerly to the lower discipline in order to achieve the higher. Wagner did it when, as a young man, he copied out the complete score of Beethoven's Ninth Symphony to learn more of the technique of orchestration; Macaulay did it when as a boy he memorized all of *Paradise Lost*. But most of us are short-view thinkers and feelers; and so you have either to be frequently reminded or else prodded by artificial incentives to achievement—rewards and punishments.

Try, though, to use the system of reward and punishment as sparingly as possible—especially punishment, as it is more likely to be an external discipline. "Spare the child and spoil the rod" should be your maxim. For even the lowest discipline at least has the incentive and offers the satisfaction of good performance. That is why the curmudgeonly German I mentioned in the last chapter was not merely feared by his pupils, but respected and even loved by some. "Pretty harsh sometimes," they used to say, "But we certainly learn our Latin verbs. We *get* something out of that class." What do they get? A sense of mastery. They may never learn to read Virgil appreciatively, but they have the satisfaction, for what it is worth, of having done a job well. Some of them may even get a good flying start toward an appreciation of Virgil. That is a better incentive than a rod, anyway, and it is also the goal that the old gentleman would have told you he had in mind for all; but it would have been a goal too few would ever reach to make his classes represent economically sound education. And none of his pupils—not even those who would reach the ultimate goal—would be able to have it in mind during the first year.

No, he should have done better than that. He should have known that the study of even elementary Latin can be a discipline in semantics (a word he probably had never heard of), in learning the genius of a people through its language, and in mastering elements of language history. These objectives he should have held in mind and presented to his pupils. They would have given more point to the class than a drill in "squads right" has—and they might have made it more interesting as well. Starting perhaps with the low discipline of meaningless drill, he might have led on to the higher ones till, after several years, he achieved his object of "appreciating" Virgil—itself a discipline, if properly undertaken, that includes all the others and more.

Whatever the subject, the higher disciplines should always be kept in mind. While learning a subject, it is hard to keep the long-view discipline in your own mind, but once having learned it, it is easy enough to do so for someone else. That is one of the chief functions of the teacher, and it ought to affect every day of your work. English composition is part of the art of communication and correct spelling therefore is probably a necessary, if low, discipline—but not the spelling of words a child will never use in communication. Learning geography should mean learning about the world in which we live, and therefore a verbatim and meaningless babble of definitions is never enough. The old-fashioned, drill sergeant type of teacher was pleased if a child could repeat that "an island is a body of land completely surrounded by water." The newer type of teacher merely starts with that. He wants the child to know what it means to live on an island, how life is affected on Manhattan or Stockholm or Venice by their being completely surrounded by water, how this little definition affects the story of *Treasure Island*. Not only does this sort of discussion interest pupils; it usually makes them remember the definitions much longer.

Remember that it is you, the teacher, who are responsible for the disciplines of learning just as surely as you are responsible for the discipline of keeping the class in order. It is you who are responsible for arousing and guiding the interests that will constitute the pupils' higher, inner discipline. That is why it is so important for you to be a master of your subject, not just a day ahead of the class in the textbook. If your own interest in your subject is passionate, if your knowledge is deep and wide, and if you can communicate that interest and use that knowledge, there will be no problem of the old-fashioned sort of discipline. That problem will be forgotten by both yourself and your pupils, and the business of learning will become the high adventure that it ought to be.